PENGUIN BOOKS

Cosmopolitan How to Get Ahead in Your Career

Suzanne King is an experienced journalist who has worked on a number of magazines, including *Cosmopolitan* (of which she is a former Careers Editor), *She* and *Radio Times*. Now a freelance writer and commissioning editor, she is also series editor of the *Cosmopolitan* Career Guides, author of the *Cosmopolitan Guide to Working in Journalism and Publishing* and co-author of the *Cosmopolitan Guide to the Big Trip*, both of which are published or forthcoming in Penguin.

COSMOPOLITAN
How to **Get Ahead in Your Career**

SUZANNE KING

PENGUIN BOOKS

PENGUIN BOOKS

Published by the Penguin Group
Penguin Books Ltd, 27 Wrights Lane, London W8 5TZ, England
Penguin Books USA Inc., 375 Hudson Street, New York 10014, USA
Penguin Books Australia Ltd, Ringwood, Victoria, Australia
Penguin Books Canada Ltd, 10 Alcorn Avenue, Toronto, Ontario, Canada M4V 3B2
Penguin Books (NZ) Ltd, 182–190 Wairau Road, Auckland 10, New Zealand

Penguin Books Ltd, Registered Offices: Harmondsworth, Middlesex, England

First published 1996
10 9 8 7 6 5 4 3 2 1

Copyright © The National Magazine Company, 1996
All rights reserved

The expression Cosmopolitan is the trade mark of The National Magazine
Company Limited and The Hearst Corporation, registered in the UK and the
USA, and other principal countries of the world, and is the absolute property of
The National Magazine Company Limited and The Hearst Corporation. The use
of this trade mark other than with the express permission of The National
Magazine Company or The Hearst Corporation is strictly prohibited.

The moral right of the author has been asserted

Set in 10½/13pt Monotype Baskerville
Typeset by Datix International Limited, Bungay, Suffolk
Printed in England by Clays Ltd, St Ives plc

Except in the United States of America, this book is sold subject
to the condition that it shall not, by way of trade or otherwise, be lent,
re-sold, hired out, or otherwise circulated without the publisher's
prior consent in any form of binding or cover other than that in
which it is published and without a similar condition including this
condition being imposed on the subsequent purchaser

Contents

STARTING OUT

Chapter 1 / **Choosing a Career** 1

Chapter 2 / **Hunting Out the Vacancies** 5

Chapter 3 / **Preparing Job Applications** 10

Chapter 4 / **How to Handle Interviews** 17

Chapter 5 / **Making the Most of Work Experience** 30

KEY BUSINESS SKILLS

Chapter 6 / **Verbal Communication Skills** 33

Chapter 7 / **Effective Business Writing** 37

Chapter 8 / **Telephone Techniques** 41

Chapter 9 / **Leadership** 46

Chapter 10 / **How to Manage Meetings** 52

Chapter 11 / **Time Management** 57

Chapter 12 / **How to Organize and Prioritize** 63

Chapter 13 / **Negotiation** 69

Chapter 14 / **Delegation** 73

Chapter 15 / **Mastering Public Speaking** 78

GETTING AHEAD

Chapter 16 / **Learning to Assert Yourself** 85

Chapter 17 / **What Makes You Promotable?** 91

Chapter 18 / **Getting a Pay Rise** 99

Chapter 19 / **Dealing with Difficult People** 102

Chapter 20 / **Keeping on Track of Your Career Goals** 108

Chapter 21 / **Handling Stress** 114

Chapter 22 / **Workplace Health** 118

Chapter 23 / **The Importance of Image** 122

Chapter 24 / **Business Travel and Entertaining** 126

Chapter 25 / **Setting Up Your Own Business** 129

Chapter 26 / **Changing Career** 138

STARTING OUT

Chapter 1 / **Choosing a Career**

Choosing what sort of job you want to do is the hardest of all career decisions. When you're entering the job market for the first time, there are so many different possibilities that it can be hard to know where to begin. The important thing is not to make any rash decisions: work is going to occupy most of your day for the next thirty or forty years, so it's worth taking time and care over making the right choice.

Assess Yourself

The first step before applying for any job is to start with some self-assessment. Take a long, hard look at yourself, your personality, talents, likes and dislikes. Are you a loner, happy to work on your own, or do you prefer the social element of working as part of a team? Would you be content to follow another person's lead or are you keen to make the rules yourself? Do you crave security and routine or would you thrive on change and challenge? Neither is right or wrong but what is important is that you have a clear idea of what will make you happiest.

Now start thinking about the sort of values that will be important to you in choosing what kind of job you do. Do you want to work in an office or outdoors? Do you want to be involved in manufacturing an end product or in providing services for other people? Do you want to go into something that will offer opportunities for being self-employed eventually or will you be happiest working for someone else? Is a large salary vitally important to you or do other considerations take precedence? Would you mind wearing a uniform or is it important to you to have freedom in what you wear?

Think, too, about whether you want to work for a small company or a large one. In a small one you will have more opportunity to learn about many different aspects of the business and get more all-round experience – but there will probably be limited training and promotion prospects. A large company may have greater chances of training and promotion, more job security, and offer opportunities to work in different cities or even countries – but you'll probably get narrower experience and it can be frustrating and isolating being a small cog in a big machine.

One way to take stock of yourself is to take four sheets of paper. Head the first one 'Work Values', the second 'Core Skills', the third 'Personal Interests' and the fourth 'Personal Qualities'. On the first sheet, list all the things about work that are important to you; this may include salary, power, variety, friendship of colleagues, independence, status, creativity, flexibility, security, chances for advancement, having long holidays, challenge, etc. Now highlight the five items from the list that are *most* important to you.

On your second sheet, list all the skills you hold; this means things like report-writing, designing, organizing conferences, talking, training others, selling, problem-solving, negotiating, having ideas, anticipating others' needs, etc. (You don't necessarily need to have acquired these skills in a work environment; they may have come through voluntary work or as part of your studies.) Then select the five skills you consider to be your best.

Third, under 'Personal Interests', list all the things that you really enjoy doing, both at work and in the rest of your life. The list might include travelling, doing research, meeting new people, solving problems, supervising others, working variable hours, playing sport, writing, convincing people to buy things, using a computer. Again, pick out the five items that give you *most* pleasure.

On your final sheet, list all the positive words and phrases you can think of to describe yourself; for example: resourceful, flexible, friendly, loyal, intelligent, honest, helpful, good memory, sympathetic, determined, hardworking, funny. Then pick out the five qualities that you think will be of most use in your job search.

Transfer your top five from each list on to a separate sheet of paper, to give you a framework for your job search. Now it's time to start looking for the sort of jobs that include or could make use of these elements.

Doing Your Homework

The first step in finding an area of work that fits in with your ambitions and aspirations and will best suit your talents and needs is to do some research. Go to the library and look through careers reference books, such as the annual handbook *Occupations* (published by COIC), for some ideas of which job areas might appeal. Draw up a shortlist of jobs that seem to fit the bill, select a couple that interest you most and find out more about those in-depth. Check out careers guides to particular fields, contact trade associations for any information leaflets, read specialist professional journals, enrol on relevant courses and go to talks and seminars.

The best way to find out what a particular job is like is to talk to people who do it, so muster all your courage and call people in your target area and ask if they would be prepared to chat to you for fifteen to twenty minutes about their work. The worst they can do is say no (and inevitably some will say they're too busy to talk), but you may also be pleasantly surprised by the number of people who'll be happy to spare you some time if your approach is pleasant. Most people *love* to talk about themselves and the sort of insider information they supply can be invaluable.

Choose your time well when you ring and take the person's job into account: the producer of a live television show, for example, won't want to hear from you minutes before the programme goes on air; a restaurant manager won't be able to talk over lunchtime. Make it clear that you're just interested in finding out more about a particular area of work and are not expecting to be offered a job. Before you talk to them, prepare yourself by doing some background research: try to find out a bit about them and their careers before you go, and think about the information you need to know and the sort of questions to ask. As well as asking them what their work involves, you could sound them out about the state of the industry at the moment, trends in the way things are going, or what employers look for. And before you leave, ask if they can suggest other people in the industry who might be happy to talk to you. Don't abuse their generosity: if you asked for fifteen minutes of their time, then try not to take up more unless they're obviously happy to carry on. And remember to write a thank-you letter soon after.

If all your research indicates that there are obvious gaps in your training, knowledge or experience, then do something about it, whether it's enrolling on a word-processing course or attending industry conferences. As well as improving your skills base, you'll also be providing an employer with a positive demonstration of your commitment and enthusiasm.

If you feel you need more detailed guidance, consider investing in a job-hunting work book such as *What Color is Your Parachute?* by Richard Nelson Bolles (Ten Speed Press), *How to Find the Perfect Job* and *Perfect Job Search Strategies* by Tom Jackson (Piatkus) or *Which Way Now?* by Bridget Wright (Piatkus). Each of these takes you step by step through the process of choosing a direction and finding a job – and gives your confidence a boost while you're at it.

Chapter 2 / **Hunting Out the Vacancies**

The most obvious way to find out about job vacancies is via the recruitment advertising sections of newspapers. National newspapers are probably better for senior level vacancies; local newspapers carry more ads for lower level jobs. Many papers specialize in particular types of jobs on particular days (see box, p. 6).

Trade journals specializing in your field of interest can also be a good source of job ads. You could also consider using a specialist recruitment agency. The Federation of Recruitment and Employment Services (36–38 Mortimer Street, London W1N 7RB; 0171-323 4300) can provide list of agencies working in particular fields, some free of charge, others for a fee. You can also check in *Yellow Pages* under Employment Agencies and Consultants. If you have secretarial skills, you could try getting temping work in the sort of organizations you're interested in; this will give you the chance to ask about permanent vacancies as well as an idea of what the companies are like and how they work.

When you see a job ad that interests you, study it carefully. What sort of qualities and experience do you think the interviewer is looking for? How can you demonstrate that you have them? Don't be afraid to apply for a job just because you don't have every single quality asked for in the ad – employers know that there is rarely such a creature as the totally perfect candidate. As long as you meet *most* of the requirements, and definitely the essential ones, you're in with a chance. It isn't necessarily the most qualified person who gets a job, but the person who prepares and sells herself best; the one who has really thought out her application and covering letter, presented them well, prepared for interview and performed well on the day.

Newspaper recruitment ads

The Times
Monday: Education; La Crème de la Crème (secretarial)
Tuesday: Legal Appointments
Wednesday: Media, Sales & Marketing; La Crème de la Crème
Thursday: Accountancy & Finance; Senior/Management; General; La Crème de la Crème; Public & Healthcare

Guardian
Monday: Creative, Media & Marketing; Sales; Secretarial
Tuesday: Education; Senior Appointments; Universities; Research; TEFL; Social Services; Community Work
Wednesday: Society (environment, social change, health, housing, local government, charities, public, senior appointments)
Thursday: Computing, Science & Technology; Commercial; Graduates
Saturday: The week's job ads repeated in the Careers Supplement

Daily Telegraph
Monday: Business & Franchise Opportunities
Wednesday: Educational
Thursday: General (including management, sales, engineering)

Independent
Tuesday: Media, Marketing & Sales
Thursday: Education, General, Graduate, Public

Daily Mail
Monday: Franchises
Thursday: Sales, Printing & Publishing

Daily Express
Monday: Franchises, Business Opportunities
Tuesday: Training & Tuition; General
Thursday: Engineering & Technical; Sales

Financial Times
Wednesday: Sales & Marketing

Sunday Times
General

Job ad jargon

OTE	on-target earnings
PQE	post-qualifications experience
PRPS	profit related pay scheme
AAE	according to age and experience
PA	per annum
pro rata	in proportion (if the pay is given as £12,000 pro rata, that means that is what the annual salary would be; but if the job is for six months only you would get half of that; or if it's permanent but for only three days a week, you would get three-fifths)
£10k	£10,000
blue chip co.	company with a reliable, prestigious reputation
IT	information technology
FMCG	fast moving consumer goods
comm	commission
f/t	full-time
p/t	part-time
neg	negotiable
tba/tbc	to be announced/to be confirmed
o/t	overtime

Creative Job Search

The trouble with newspaper job ads, of course, is that millions of others are scouring them along with you. And sitting back and waiting for the perfect ad to appear in the paper could take years – so don't. Go out looking instead. It's been estimated that only 10 per cent of people get jobs by answering newspaper ads, and many employers try to cut costs and avoid a deluge of applications by relying on word of mouth to find suitable candidates, especially in some of the most sought-after careers such as those in the media.

Read the specialist press and the business pages of the newspapers so that you'll know when companies are expanding or have won new contracts and might therefore be looking to recruit more staff.

Networking is one of the best ways of finding a job, so make sure that all your friends, colleagues, ex-colleagues and relatives know that you're looking for work. Contacts in your prospective industry or company are your best job-hunting asset: if anyone you know is employed by an organization you want to work for, ask them to keep an ear to the ground and an eye on in-house noticeboards and magazines to find out if any jobs are going. Many companies advertise jobs internally first, and some offer cash incentives to staff who can help them fill a vacancy without having to resort to the expense and trouble of national newspaper advertising.

Once you have a target organization in mind, call to find out the name of the person in charge of the department, and write directly to them – rather than to Personnel or Human Resources – and specify the kind of work you're looking for. Your letter may then be passed on to Personnel but not before it's been seen by the person who really makes the decisions about whom to employ. Once you've made the initial contact, follow it up. Don't make a nuisance of yourself by nagging them every week, but maybe every few months, or if you hear of movement within the company, call and remind them that you would still be interested in working for them.

Don't just whack off job applications indiscriminately: it's better to spend time on a few well-prepared applications than to waste time and money applying for posts you're not suitable for, don't really want or haven't bothered to research properly. It's important to keep up some momentum, so try to do *something* every day – send off at least one on-spec application, make one phone call to find more information, take one trip to the library to use a reference book. It might help to get you motivated if you team up with a friend who's job hunting too, so that you can encourage and support each other and exchange ideas and feedback.

Make no mistake: finding a job is hard work and you'll need resilience, persistence and determination. Even some junior roles attract hundreds of applicants so it could take some time (and a few rejections) before you finally strike it lucky. However, the harder you work at it, the better you'll get.

Chapter 3 / **Preparing Job Applications**

CVs

The purpose of a CV is to get you an interview – and that applies whether you're writing to an employer on spec or applying for an advertised vacancy. The idea is to make it a tempting taster so that they'll want to find out more. It's not meant to tell the whole story of your life and, unless you work in a very technical or academic field, should never be more than two sides long – no employer is going to want to read more than that. For recent graduates, one page is enough. Have a basic CV always ready, but adapt it for each job you apply for, emphasizing or downplaying different aspects as relevant. The fact that you spent several vacations working in a local clothes shop may be of limited interest if you're applying for a job as a research scientist, but if you're being interviewed by a department store it could show that you have relevant experience and knowledge of the industry.

There are many different styles of CV and it's largely a question of taste which you choose. The traditional and most widely recognized CV is one that follows a chronological format. This is best for those who have followed a straight career path, and are planning to continue in the same direction. After your basic personal details (name, address, telephone number, date of birth, nationality), give your career history, starting with your current or most recent job, and working backwards. State the job title, company name and period of employment, give a brief job description and mention any special achievements. Describe your current post in most detail; be more succinct about any before that. After Career History, list Educational Qualifications, again working backwards. You may also wish to include Other

Information (e.g. driving licence, foreign languages, computer skills).

Alternatively, you could opt for a functional/skills CV. It's not as common but is useful if you have had frequent job changes, are trying to change career direction or have a limited career history but have acquired relevant skills and experience in other areas such as voluntary work or work experience. It also takes the emphasis off any gaps. Under headings such as Administrative Abilities or Communication Skills, summarize your experience in those areas. If you're applying for an advertised job, make sure you match your headings to the qualities asked for in the ad. Voluntary work is a particularly good source of transferable skills: charity fund-raising shows evidence of organizational and marketing skills; teaching adult literacy or English as a second language calls for effective communication skills and an ability to motivate others; chairing the university entertainments committee will probably have brought you experience in delegation, organization and chairing meetings, all of which fit nicely under Management Skills.

Your third option is a targeted CV, best used when you're applying for jobs on spec rather than in response to specific advertisements. The emphasis is on aiming for a particular position and explaining why you're qualified for it. Under the heading Job Target state the post you're aiming for, e.g. production manager for a leading clothes manufacturer. Then, under headings such as Capabilities, Accomplishments or Skills and Achievements, list your skills and talents which relate to your prospective position and what you've done so far that shows you'd be able to perform in the job. ('Prepared customer orders; determined needs and quantities; managed product cost analyses'.) Further headings should include Work Experience and Education, as on a chronological CV.

Whichever format you choose, there are certain basic rules to follow:
- Use good quality white or off-white paper. Avoid anything fancy or gimmicky. No coloured paper, no fiddly folders, no confusing graphics. Yes, green paper might make you stand out – but it's

just as likely to irritate the employer. There's a fine line between creative and cringeworthy: better to play safe.
- It must look good. Make the layout as clear and accessible as possible, using a clear, easy-to-read typeface. Use bold and italic typefaces, capital letters, bullet points, underlining, etc., to make it clear – but don't go mad. Leave plenty of white space, with wide margins and spaces between sections, rather than cramping everything together.
- Avoid long sentences. An employer wants to see the facts at a glance and won't be impressed by rambling prose. Keep phrases short, punchy and active, starting with a verb: 'developed new sales strategy', 'managed team of ten'. You don't need to say 'I' every time – who else would you be talking about in your CV?
- Condense, condense, condense. Cut out anything that's not essential, such as addresses of employers or educational institutions.
- A CV should always be typed – and *well* typed. Do it on a word processor with a high quality printer. If you can't type or don't have access to a machine, get someone who knows how to type properly to do it for you – ask a friend or pay to have it done. A badly typed CV is almost as off-putting as a handwritten one.
- There's no need to include referees on a CV unless you have such stunningly good ones that it would impress an employer. If an employer needs them, she'll ask. Never give anyone's name as a referee without checking with them first.
- Check, double check and triple check your CV – then give it to a friend to check again. Mistakes will count against you.
- Eliminate the negative. If your grades were low, leave them out (but have an answer ready if you're asked about them at interview). A CV is a selling document, not the place to advertise every exam you've ever failed or career setback you've faced.
- Don't include current salary details unless asked to do so. People will make certain assumptions about you and your worth if you give them specific figures and you could put yourself out of the running by earning too little or too much. Plenty of time to talk money later.

- Most employers agree that using a specialist CV-writing service is unnecessary and many actively dislike CVs designed by specialist consultancies, so try to do it yourself.
- Remember to adapt your CV as the years go on, adding, cutting and rewriting. For example, the further away you get from your schooldays, the less relevent your O levels or GCSEs become, so gradually prune back the details as more relevant experience supersedes them ('University of Liverpool, 1988–1992, BA (Hons) French and German 2:2, 3 A levels, 9 GCSEs' is all you need once you're already working). Nor do you need to carry on putting down the Saturday job you did when you were sixteen.
- Include interests and hobbies if you have little work experience as yet; otherwise leave them out unless they demonstrate a skill or quality relevant to the job or are so astonishing or unusual that they will intrigue the interviewer.
- If applying for jobs abroad, enclose a passport photograph of yourself – it's far more common to do this in other European countries than it is here.
- If you're responding to a job ad, make sure that the skills you highlight in your CV match those specified in the ad.

Positive/active words that stand out on CVs

achieved • administered • analysed • built • capable
competent • communicated • consistent • controlled
co-ordinated • created • designed • developed • directed
economical • effective • efficient • established • expanded
experienced • guided • implemented • improved
initiated • increased • introduced • led • managed
monitored • organized • participated • positive • processed
produced • professional • proficient • profitable
qualified • repaired • resourceful • responsible • skilled
sold • specialized • stable • successful • supervised
trained • versatile • volunteered

- Extra skills such as computer literacy and foreign languages are valuable – but don't make them up to impress. If you claim to have fluent French, for example, you could find an interviewer asking you some questions in that language and you'll look pretty stupid if you don't understand.

The Covering Letter

Never send off a CV or application form without a covering letter or you'll miss a great opportunity to sell yourself. If you have a glowing testimonial or letter of recommendation from a former employer, you should enclose that too. Keep your letter short and to the point: it should fit on to one sheet, preferably on the same high-quality paper as your CV.

- Put your address in the top right-hand corner of the letter or centred at the top of the page, and the date and address of the person you're sending it to below that on the left-hand side. Make sure you address the letter to someone by name rather than 'the Personnel Officer' or 'Dear Sir/Madam'. Call the company first to find out, and always check if you're not sure how to spell the name. The correct ending to a letter addressed to a person by name is 'Yours sincerely' ('Yours faithfully' is only used when the addressee is Dear Sir or Dear Madam).
- Make sure the letter is tidy, well written and includes all the essential information – if there are lots of applicants for a job, it's easy to start by discarding the ones whose replies are scruffy or ill-prepared. Typing looks smarter, unless the employer specifically requests a handwritten letter, in which case draft it on a rough piece of paper first so that you can write the final letter without mistakes. Use blue or (preferably) black ink; other colours are generally frowned upon and green ink is considered the trademark of a loony.
- Whatever job you're applying for, it's important that your spelling, grammar and punctuation should be correct. If you're not sure, ask someone else to look it over for you. Use the

spelling or grammar check on your computer if you have one.
- Keep the language simple. Many people make the mistake of using over-formal, flowery phrases, which just sound stilted and unnatural.
- Explain why you are writing. If you're applying for a specific job, either in response to an ad or a word-of-mouth vacancy, say how you heard about the position, where and when. If a reference number was given, be sure to include it. If you're writing at the suggestion of someone the employer knows personally or someone who is well known in the field, then mention it straight away. For example: 'Jane Smith at Company X suggested that I write to you about my idea for . . .'; 'John Brown mentioned that you were looking for salespeople for your new branch.'
- State briefly why you are a strong candidate and emphasize what you have to offer the employer: not 'I've always wanted to work in marketing' but 'I have acquired the following skills which I believe would be of value to your company . . .'
- Draw attention to the relevant bits of your CV but don't go into details. Save that for the interview.
- Always target your letter to each particular company you write to. Don't just photocopy a standard letter – there's nothing more off-putting than receiving a letter that is obviously being mailed to hundreds of companies with no particular interest. If you have access to a computer, it's hardly any trouble to modify.
- Don't write a fabulous letter, then ruin the effect by cramming it into a tiny little envelope. Your paper should never be folded more than twice, so make sure your envelope is A4, A5 or 220 × 110 mm.

Application Forms

Many companies, especially large ones, ask all job applicants to fill in an application form rather than sending in a CV. It makes it easier for them to find the information they need to know quickly, which is invaluable when dealing with large numbers of people.

Even if you've already submitted a CV, you should complete an application form if one is sent to you.

- Photocopy the blank form and do a rough version of your answers on the photocopy first. Then, once you're happy with it, copy them on to the original.
- Complete all sections, however irrelevant they might seem. Don't leave the Further Information box blank – you'll miss a chance to shine and say things you haven't had the opportunity to say elsewhere. Look back at the job ad to see what they were asking for and if you haven't been able to prove how well you match the description anywhere else, now's your chance.
- Write legibly and in black ink: the form will probably be photocopied and blue ink doesn't photocopy well.
- Take a copy of the finished form to reread before the interview. It's also a useful reference for the next time you have one to fill in and means you don't have to start again from scratch.

If you've written off for a job, bear in mind that the employer might call you out of the blue to fix up an interview, so make sure that your phone manners are up to scratch and that you don't have a stupid message on your answering machine. It's not a bad idea to keep your CV and interview letters by the phone so you don't get caught off guard if they conduct their initial interviews this way.

Chapter 4 / **How to Handle Interviews**

Interviews can be a nerve-racking experience, especially for first-time job hunters or those returning to work after a break and perhaps feeling less than confident. And the more you want the job, the worse it is. However, nerves come, in a large part, from feeling unready and unprepared, so the more you plan ahead, the better your chances and the better you'll feel on the day. The aim is to appear confident and in control but not cocky. Whatever kind of job you're going for, the following tips apply.

Before the Interview

- Make sure you know the industry backwards. Read the business pages of newspapers and look out for any relevant activity in the market. Dig out any trade journals that will fill you in on the background (look in a book like *BRAD*, *PiMS* or *Willings Press Guide* for lists of trade titles; your local reference library should have copies). Trade bodies or federations may have information leaflets. The more senior the job you're aiming for, the more important it is to be well informed and up-to-date about issues affecting the industry.
- You should be able to make intelligent, informed comments on the company itself and its area of work, so do some homework before the interview and find out as much as possible about it. How big is it? Who are its main competitors? Who are its customers? Ring the personnel department and ask if they can send you any useful literature: company reports, in-house magazines, etc. Ask friends if they know anyone in the organization who wouldn't mind chatting to you and giving you some tips. Look for

information in the local reference library or Chamber of Commerce, or contact a business school and ask if you can use their library. Research may be time-consuming but it's worth it: it shows initiative and motivation and will give you a great advantage over candidates who haven't bothered. If you're ignorant about the company's work, then you're obviously not that interested in them or, presumably, the job. Don't be careless: confusing the company's products with those of a rival won't win you any friends.

- Read the newspapers or keep up with the news on TV or radio for a few weeks before the interview so that you're well aware of current affairs and how they might affect the company's business.
- If you're in work already, prepare a clear, succinct précis of your job and be prepared to answer questions on any aspect of it. Past performance is the main thing employers have to rely on when it comes to assessing how well you would do with them so make sure you feed them relevant examples of your experience. How have you shown initiative, drive, leadership qualities, reliability, supervisory or cost-cutting skills, management ability, organizational flair? How have you moved on since you joined your company? Can you work well under pressure or adapt to changing conditions? What new technology skills do you have?
- If you're going for your first job after school or university, you're unlikely to have much work experience, but you need to show employers that there's more to your life than books and bars. It's even more important, therefore, to look carefully at your experience and other areas of your life for evidence of what you have to offer employers. Did you have involvement in school and university societies and clubs that show your skills in various areas? Did you participate in team sports? Write for the school magazine? Handle accounts as treasurer of the entertainments committee? Serve on a hall of residence committee? Deliver seminars? Undertake extensive or unusual travel during vacations? Act as a fund-raiser for your local Friends of the Earth branch? Have you done voluntary work, served time on a local community committee, been involved in an advisory board? Have you done any work placements during the holidays? Be prepared to answer questions

about why you did these things and what you feel you've gained from them.

- Imagine you've been given the job you're going for. What would you do to increase sales, make sure that deadlines are being met, improve the way of working? Consider the sort of problems they're likely to be facing and how you could help solve them.
- Read the job advertisement/description carefully and think closely about what sort of qualities and experience you think the interviewer will be looking for. How can you demonstrate that you have them?
- The sorts of things the interviewer wants to know are: are you dependable, reliable, honest, a good team-worker, confident, decisive, co-operative, responsible, enthusiastic, organized, etc? And what evidence can you provide to prove it?
- Rehearse your answers and the points you're keen to make. If you're a bit rusty at interviews try to run the whole thing through with a more practised friend beforehand, getting her to play the interviewer. She may come up with more possible questions you hadn't thought of. You may feel silly at first but it *will* help. Ask for honest feedback and don't get upset or defensive if there are negative points – that will discourage further comment. Don't over-rehearse or you'll end up sounding stilted and unnatural when you want to appear spontaneous and relaxed.
- You don't always get much notice of an interview so don't leave all your preparation until the letter arrives. Start thinking about it when you first apply.
- Don't spend so long worrying about the questions you'll be asked that you forget the basics. Get plenty of sleep the night before the interview. Work out in advance how you're going to get there and how long it will take – and allow extra time for delays. Make sure a couple of days ahead that your clothes are clean and ready.

On the Day

Getting in the Mood

- Be positive! If you've been asked for an interview, they're obviously interested in you. To get to this stage you've probably already beaten hundreds of others and may be on a short list of somewhere between six and twelve. You wouldn't have been invited for interview if the employer didn't already believe you are capable of the job – all you have to do is prove it.
- Remember the poor interviewer too. Far from being out to get you, she wants nothing more than to like you and to find you're the very person they need – otherwise she's going to have to carry on and on doing more interviews.
- Do anything to help boost your confidence: read a favourite poem or inspirational book on the way to the interview; listen to 'up' music on your Walkman; remind yourself of all the times you've triumphed against the odds or all the things you've done that make you feel proud.
- Reread your letter/CV/application form and be ready to answer questions on anything you've included. Take copies with you in case the interviewer has mislaid them.
- Read a newspaper on the morning of the interview in case you're asked about topical issues.
- If you're wearing a skirt, take a spare pair of tights with you. Take a needle and cotton (for emergency repairs), phonecard and small change (for parking or phone calls). Make sure you have the company's phone number so you can call in an emergency. And don't forget to take their address.
- Just turning up gives you a head start! One employer who recently arranged to interview twenty applicants referred by the local job centre was amazed when only twelve of them actually turned up – and only three of those were on time.
- Set out in plenty of time and aim to arrive ten to fifteen minutes

early. Don't expect buses or trains to be on time, or assume that you'll find a parking space easily. Use your waiting time to watch the people around you, read any internal notice-boards or in-house newsletters, and generally try to get a feel for the place. If you're nervous, try a few relaxation exercises – rolling your shoulders, breathing deeply, etc.
- Don't smoke or drink shortly before the interview – smelling of tobacco or alcohol isn't going to impress any interviewer.

Looking the Part

Never underestimate the importance of appearance. Research has shown that an interviewer's impression of you will be made up of 55 per cent on how you look, 38 per cent on how you sound and only 7 per cent on what you say. First impressions are all-important – they're quickly formed and hard to change, and though your interview might last an hour, a decision has probably been largely made within the first four or five minutes.
- Your clothes don't need to be expensive – nobody expects someone fresh out of college to waltz in in Armani – but they must be presentable and clean. Make sure they're comfortable, too: you can't concentrate on the interview if you're too busy worrying about wayward buttons or squirming around because your skirt's too tight.
- Dress appropriately for the organization: if you're going for a bank job, a smart suit would probably be best, but if you're applying for work in the media, a suit might give a misleading impression of someone formal and stiff so something more casual might go down better. As a general rule, though, think smart rather than trendy. Some experts recommend going to watch staff leaving or entering the workplace, so that you get an idea of the corporate image and tailor your interview outfit accordingly (same kind of clothes but a bit smarter).
- Shoes should be polished. Heels look smarter than flat – but not *too* high
- Studies suggest that wearing light, natural make-up rather than

none at all increases your chances of success by 20 per cent. Employers are also likely to think you're worth more money. It also seems that if you want to be taken seriously the best hairstyle is short and sleek. If you have long hair, tie it back or wear it up.
- Keep perfume, if you must wear any, discreet. Don't wear jangly bangles or dangly earrings that you'll be tempted to play with.
- Don't smoke, even if invited to do so – it looks messy. And, unless you're ultra-relaxed, it might be as well to refuse any offers of tea or coffee: they just provide more scope for disaster.
- Make sure you look smart and cool as you walk through the interview-room door. Don't go in clutching carrier bags of shopping or a dripping wet coat and umbrella; leave any encumbrances with the receptionist to look after. Don't put your bag on the desk.
- Try to appear confident, even if you're quaking inside, and avoid betraying yourself with negative body language. Walk in confidently rather than creeping apologetically round the door and sit upright but relaxed in the chair, not hunched over or slumped. Leaning slightly forward shows attention and interest. Look the interviewer in the eye – looking down or away suggests nervousness or even dishonesty – but don't fix her with an unwavering stare. Keep your arms and legs uncrossed, don't shift around in your seat and try not to fiddle with jewellery or your hair. Merely sitting comfortably gives you the desired appearance of being poised, calm and confident.
- Speak up (there's nothing more irritating than having to ask people to repeat themselves all the time) and, if you tend to gabble when nervous, make a conscious effort to speak more slowly. Try to sound enthusiastic and interested.
- However nervous you feel, *smile*! Most interviewers base their final decisions on gut feeling, and it's only natural that they will warm more to someone who appears relaxed and friendly. After all, they want to employ someone they can get on with, someone who will be pleasant to work with as well as able to do the job. As an added bonus, smiling will help relax your facial muscles and relieve some of that tension that's bound to be building up.

- Don't save your best behaviour for the interviewer alone: be just as pleasant to the receptionist and anyone else you make contact with – they may be asked for their impressions.

In the Interview

- If the interviewer starts by asking you a few general questions, like how your journey to the interview was, remember she's only trying to put you at your ease and don't go into great detail.
- A bit of humour or wit at appropriate moments will make you more memorable to an interviewer and provide light relief in what is, for her, probably a rather dull day of grilling nervous candidates.
- Concentrate on listening properly to what the interviewer is saying, rather than fretting about how you're doing and what she might ask next. If you miss something or are confused by a question, it's better to ask for clarification than to waffle on with an inappropriate answer. Keep your answers relevant.
- It's normal to play up your good points and try to skim over the bad ones but you don't want to look as if you have something to hide. If the interviewer asks about any area you'd hoped to avoid (a previous redundancy, say, or a series of short-term jobs), answer briefly but honestly.
- If you're asked why you want to leave your current job, don't just say you're bored or want more money, even if it's true. Couch your reasons in more positive terms: not 'I'm bored' but 'I've learned a great deal in the job but have now reached a stage where there are no immediate promotion prospects and I'm ready to tackle new challenges and to take on more responsibility.' Don't ever launch into a complaint about how awful your present employer is, even if it's true: you'll just sound like a whinger.
- Be specific in your answers. If you're asked how you would handle situation X, for example, say – if you can – how you dealt successfully with a similar situation in the past.
- Expect to be asked about your personal life and leisure interests as well as strictly work issues. It may seem irrelevant to you, but

any involvement in local community activity, voluntary work, amateur dramatics, school and university societies, etc., could be interesting to potential employers and will help them to put together a picture of you as a complete person. For example, leading roles in amateur dramatic productions suggest confidence, an outgoing nature and a good memory. Consider what it is about your leisure activities or hobbies that appeals to you – interviewers often ask about these things and it can be hard to think of a good answer off the top of your head.

- Be ready to explain why you're interested in this job. That may sound obvious but it's surprising how many people don't think it through and end up floundering. It's not enough to say it's because the location is convenient for you or the holiday allowance is very generous.

- Straightforward questions about your studies, qualifications or job history are relatively easy to answer and you should certainly expect to be asked any of the questions in the box opposite. Most interviewers aren't out to trap you or make you feel uncomfortable but there are always one or two who like to spring on you horrors such as 'How would your best friend/worst enemy/colleagues describe you?' or 'What are your strengths/weaknesses?' You're unlikely to think of something suitable on the spot so it helps to think ahead and have examples prepared. *Great Answers to Tough Interview Questions* by Martin John Yate (Kogan Page) has some excellent tips on how to answer potential clangers.

- If you've filled in an application form, it's quite likely that some of the interview will be spent expanding on the information there.

- Employers usually take up references so don't lie about something a referee might be asked to corroborate.

- Be guarded about criticizing former employers – the interviewer may wonder if you'll do the same to them one day.

- Panel or board interviews can be especially daunting but at least you're less at the whim of one person's likes and dislikes. Sit where you can see everyone and they can all see you – if the chair's in the wrong place, move it. Members of the panel usually take it in turns to ask questions and you should watch the questioner as she

Questions you're likely to be asked

Tell me about yourself.
What makes you right for this job?
Why do you want to work for us?
What do you like/dislike in your current job?
Why do you want to leave your current job?
Where do you see yourself in five years' time?
Tell me all about your current job.
What do you think of the company/product? What changes would you make?
What computer systems have you worked on?
How do you feel about working long hours?
Remember: questions may not be phrased in exactly the same way, so don't rehearse entire off-pat answers.

---

talks to you, then address your answers mainly to her, but include the other panel members with occasional eye contact. Return your gaze to the chairperson at the end. If possible, find out in advance who the members of the panel will be, so you have some idea of what to expect. Try to memorize their names and be equally polite and friendly to all members whatever their manner. When it is your turn to ask questions, direct them to the chair, who can redirect them to the appropriate member of the panel.

• Don't blurt out answers when you're nervous: if you're asked something tricky it's OK to pause slightly while you frame your answer.

• If there's a silence after you've given your answer to a question, don't feel you have to blunder in and fill it. Unless you have something useful to add, it's better to ask the interviewer if you've answered the question fully enough, which puts the ball firmly back in their court, and wait for the next question.

• If you're asked about your hobbies and interests, don't say anything you can't back up. If you say you're keen on the theatre, for example, expect to be asked, 'What is the best play you've seen recently?' or 'Who is your favourite playwright?'

- Remember, this is a two-way process: it's a time for you to find out about the potential employer and the job as well as vice versa, so don't miss your chance when asked if you have any questions. It also provides another opportunity for you to impress. Prepare three or four intelligent questions that demonstrate your genuine interest in the job or your familiarity with the business and the challenges facing it ('I read in *Retail Week* that ... and I was wondering how this will affect ...'). Write the questions down on an index card if you think you might forget them – it won't do any harm to bring out the list but have it conveniently to hand so you don't have to scrabble through your pockets or bag. If the interviewer doesn't offer you the chance to ask questions, then volunteer, but remember that asking too many is as bad as asking none at all: three or four pertinent ones is about right. Be sensitive about time and alert to signs of impatience in the interviewer – the next candidate is probably waiting. If all your questions have been answered during the course of the interview, then say so.
- Questions about childcare and marital status are illegal but that doesn't stop some people asking them. If you want the job, it's probably best just to assure them briefly that you can cope and wouldn't have applied for the job otherwise.
- Requests that make you look silly (like asking you to sing something) are a test of self-esteem. Refuse, politely but firmly.
- Don't leave the interview without finding out what happens next. At the end it's perfectly reasonable to ask, 'How soon can I expect to hear from you?'
- Leave salary, hours, holidays, etc., until a second interview – or until the interviewer brings the subject up. If you must ask now, choose your words carefully: for example, 'Perhaps you could tell me a little more about the terms and conditions of the job,' rather than 'So what's the salary and how much holiday will I get?'

Negotiating Your Salary

It's very un-British to talk about money, and many people will just accept whatever salary is offered in their relief at getting the job. However, the fact is that salary is almost always open to negotiation, providing you go about it in the right way.

- Before you go to an interview, you should try to find out the going rate for the job. Ask people working in the industry; contact professional associations; look at similar job ads to see if they mention money; talk to a careers officer.
- If you're asked how much you earn now, remember to take into account any perks you may have (company pension, annual bonuses or pay rise, private health insurance, interest-free travel loan, subsidized canteen, generous maternity leave, profit share, etc.).
- Always try to get the employer to mention a figure before you do, but if they ask you to say what you're looking for, don't think in terms of what you need but in terms of what the job is worth. Don't give a fixed figure, but a range: 'I'm looking for something in the high twenties' or 'I would hope for a substantial increase on the £15,000 I'm earning now.' If they give a range, don't undersell yourself: aim for the top.
- If the employer is immovable on salary, or won't go as high as you'd like, think about other areas that might be open to negotiation: for example, flexible working hours, an early salary appraisal, training opportunities, company car, etc.
- Be sure to get any agreement in writing.

After the Interview

- Assess your performance and see if there's anything you can learn from it. What went well? What went badly? If there were any questions that caught you out, brush up your answers for next time.

- If, despite all your best efforts, the interview was a disaster, don't automatically blame yourself. If you're unlucky enough to land an unpleasant or aggressive interviewer, you'll just have to write it off to experience and remind yourself that the next one can only be better. Ask yourself if you'd really want to work for an organization that treats people like that or employs such people anyway.
- However the interview went, it's a good idea to write a brief letter the next day, thanking the interviewer for seeing you, reinforcing any important points and adding any extra relevant information you might have forgotten or been unable to pass on at the time. Keep it short and sweet – just enough to nudge the interviewer's memory and show that you really are keen. Don't go over the top: sounding too smarmy or desperate will only put people off.
- If you don't hear anything within the time expected, write or call to find out the state of play. Let them know if you have other interviews/offers to consider but don't make it sound like a threat. After the initial enquiry, leave it – hassling only irritates people.
- If you're offered the job, clarify all terms and conditions before accepting. If you wait until you're in it before sorting things out, you're in a weaker position to bargain. Don't hand in your notice in your current job until you have something in writing from your new employer – a verbal offer can be withdrawn.
- If you don't get the job but are still keen to work for the company, write thanking them for taking the time to see you and saying you were sorry to be unsuccessful this time but would like to be kept on file in case of future vacancies. It wouldn't hurt to ask what the person who was appointed had that you didn't. Make it clear you're just looking for helpful feedback, not getting huffy and demanding explanations. It's not easy to do but at least it might give you something useful to take away from the experience rather than seeing it as a total failure.
- Keeping up morale is important. It can be discouraging when you apply unsuccessfully for a string of jobs, especially when your

friends are all finding their dream jobs, but don't let yourself sink into depression. Treat each interview as practice and remember that if you take great care over your letters and CVs you're already streets ahead of most applicants. Your time will come.

Chapter 5 / **Making the Most of Work Experience**

If you're a student starting to think about finding your first job, you need to start gathering skills, practical experience and training as soon as possible to give you the edge in the job hunt. Remember that come June the job market will be flooded with thousands of new school-leavers and graduates eager for work and chasing the same jobs. It may be tough, but it's no use waiting till you leave before you begin to think about your career. The earlier you start, the better so don't leave your job search to the last minute.

You have more opportunities now than you will ever have again after you leave, so don't waste them. As well as doing the obvious things, like working on the student newspaper or campus radio if you're interested in a career in journalism, make the most of any free training on offer, in computing or languages, for example, all of which can be useful skills in any field.

The one thing, however, that will impress potential employers most is relevant work experience, and as much of it as possible, so good vacation jobs are vital. If you have secretarial skills, you may be able to find temping work. The other way of getting that all-important experience – and real insider view – is by offering to work for free. A good work placement will teach you more about a job than any careers book or counsellor can and the experience gained can be more valuable than all the paper qualifications in the world when it comes to getting a permanent job. It's also a chance to make useful contacts and, if it goes well, will stand you in good stead when vacancies come up. You're unlikely to be paid but some companies will cover your expenses – look on it as an investment.

There are a few points to bear in mind if you want to get maximum benefit from a work placement.

- Lots of students look for work experience in the holidays, so you're more likely to find something if you can work during term-time. You should apply at least a couple of months in advance, as it can be difficult to get a place. When you apply, state exactly what area of work you're interested in and enclose a full CV. Give evidence of your interest, say what you hope to achieve and point out what they'll gain from having you.
- Be reliable. Even though you won't be paid a fortune (if anything at all) you should behave professionally, arriving on time and not leaving before the end of the working day.
- Be cheerful and don't sulk if the work you're given is not to your taste. Most of the work you'll be given will be thoroughly mundane (would *you* trust an inexperienced student with anything else?) but if you do the photocopying, tea-making and lunch-fetching with good grace you'll make a good impression. Do it with enthusiasm – or offer before you're asked – and you'll definitely be remembered.
- However boring the tasks you're given to do, do them all *well* – every little detail matters. Make sure any documents you type are free of spelling mistakes; don't make coffee when someone asked for tea.
- How you handle people on the phone will be noticed, so be polite, try to sound authoritative and make sure when you take messages that you get the person's name and number and note down the date and time of their call. Watch how other people deal with callers for hints on how to behave. Don't take the opportunity of the 'free' phones to call all your friends. If you must make a personal call, ask permission first.
- Try to shine – but without getting on people's nerves. This is a time to use your intuition: you should be able to feel when it's OK to talk and when everyone's so frantic that you should hold back.
- It's always better to ask questions if you're doing something you don't understand than to blunder ahead and get it wrong. But

whenever you ask a question, pay attention to the answer and write everything down so you don't irritate people by asking the same questions over and over again.
- Remember people's names: if necessary, draw yourself a little plan of the office with names by desks to jog your memory.
- Try to move around departments to get a flavour of each, rather than getting stuck in one place for the whole time.
- Use your initiative. If someone looks really busy, offer to help; if the phone rings at an empty desk, answer it. Ask if there's any outstanding filing you could help with or if the bookshelves need tidying. If there's really nothing, use the time to get some practice on the computer or to talk to people about what their jobs involve.
- If the placement was successful, ask someone you worked closely with if they would provide a reference for you. Try to get them to do it before you leave or soon after, before they forget who you are. If there's anyone you get on particularly well with, stay in contact after you leave and let them know you'd love to hear when any jobs are going within the company.

KEY BUSINESS SKILLS

Chapter 6 / **Verbal Communication Skills**

Communication is all about how you relate to other people, whether face-to-face, over the telephone or in writing. And as, for most of us, much of our working day is spent dealing with others, good communication skills are vital to career success.

Learn to Listen

Most of us flatter ourselves that we are good listeners but, in reality, we are often too preoccupied with our own worries or too busy thinking about what we want to say next to listen properly to others. On average, we ignore or forget 75 per cent of everything we hear. Yet listening is an essential and much underrated skill at work – in meetings, interviews and presentations, for example. If you can learn to *really* listen, it will improve your efficiency at work, boost your confidence and popularity and help you hold people's attention.

• Listening is all about hearing what is *not* said as well as what is, so remember to listen with your eyes as well as your ears: body language is a good guide to someone's true feelings and may not always tally with what they're saying. Try listening with your eyes closed and you'll realize how helpful it is to be able to see a speaker.

• Listen to the tone of the voice as well as to the actual words – again, there may be an underlying message.

• Make notes – not so many that you will miss half of what's

being said, but brief pointers and key words to act as a trigger to memory.
- Obvious as this may sound, you have to concentrate on what the speaker is saying. All too often people are too busy framing their own responses, in which case they're no longer attending fully.
- Don't interrupt, assume that you know what the speaker will say next or finish off her sentences: it's frustrating for her and you may be wrong.
- Keep an open mind: if your mind is cluttered with preconceived ideas, you're not a receptive listener.
- Ask questions to show that you're interested and to make sure that you understand what the speaker is saying.
- Let the other person know that you've heard and understood what they're saying by acknowledging points as they go along and then summarizing and repeating them at the end.
- Face the speaker, maintain eye contact and nod to acknowledge points made.
- Don't fidget, frown or fiddle with your hair, pen or jewellery – and never look at your watch!
- When dealing with irate people – complaining customers, for example – listening is a vital skill. Allow them to 'get it off their chest' then look for positive ways of dealing with the problem. Don't interrupt or get defensive.
- Look at people to show you're interested in them. Looking down, away or over their shoulder signals a lack of interest.

Getting Your Message Across

- Have confidence: if you relay something in an uncertain manner, people won't take it seriously. And you have to *mean* what you're saying, otherwise your lack of conviction will come across.
- Be aware of obstacles that could come between you and the person you're talking to: they can be anything from different cultural expectations to age gap to fear to relative status. Always

consider who it is you're trying to communicate with and what their particular concerns are.

- Choose the right medium for communication: writing or speech? small meeting or big presentation? Do you need to set up a meeting to discuss something or would it be better dealt with via an apparently casual comment in the lift? Should the subject be communicated via a memo or a presentation? Speaking, for example, may be better for something urgent, and writing more appropriate if you are explaining something detailed or complicated.
- Writing is more permanent and gives you more chance to consider your exact phrasing, but it is also more formal and distant, and unless you stand over someone while they read it, you can't be sure that they have. Oral communication is more personal and immediate but words can be blurted out and regretted seconds later, especially if there is disagreement.
- You'll find tips for public speaking and presentation in chapter 15, and advice on telephone techniques in chapter 8. See also chapter 16 for assertiveness advice.
- State your message as clearly as you can: don't confuse. The onus is on you to make yourself understood.
- Before you try to relay any message, make sure you fully know and understand it yourself. If you don't know what you're talking about, how can you expect anyone else to?
- Don't stand too close to other people – invading their personal space may make them feel ill at ease and under threat.
- Don't let your gestures contradict your message or you can hardly expect the other person to get your point; if you're trying to discipline someone, don't do it with a fixed grin on your face.
- Speak up: it's irritating for the other person to have to ask you to repeat things because you're whispering or mumbling.
- If your listener doesn't understand what you're saying, rephrase to make it clearer. Repeating things in the same way or in a louder voice won't help – you need to get the language right.
- Avoid umms, ers, you knows. If you're not sure whether or not you use them a lot, ask your friends.

- Most people appreciate it if you get to the point as quickly as possible; others like things to be wrapped up a bit more. Assess your listener and act accordingly.

Getting Others to Open Up

- Ask questions – and be genuinely interested in the answers. Encourage people to talk.
- Make sure your questions are open ones – that is, those that call for more than a yes/no answer. How did you do that? Why do you suppose that happened?
- Don't hog the conversation; always let other people have their say too.
- Show an interest in other people: the more you know about their life and interests apart from the purely work-related, the more you have to build a relationship on. It doesn't mean you have to interrogate them; simply asking, for example, where they spent their holiday, is the kind of thing.

Chapter 7 / **Effective Business Writing**

The way you write a letter, memo or report can affect how much impact it has: however great your ideas, it's no good if you can't communicate them successfully. Don't worry if you feel you don't have the makings of a great writer in you: business writing is a skill, like any other, that can be learned and improved with practice.

If you find business writing difficult, bear these points in mind.
- Remember your ABC. Always be Accurate, Brief and Clear.
- Before you put pen to paper, clarify your aim. *Why* are you writing? (Could this be dealt with by phone or in person?) *Who* are you writing to? (Your tone should vary depending on your reader.) *What* does your reader need to know? *How* will you write? (Are you trying to persuade? Or simply to inform?) Rudyard Kipling's verse is a useful one to remember: 'I keep six honest serving men,/They taught me all I knew,/Their names are What and Why and When/And How and Where and Who.'
- Collect your thoughts and work out a structure for the document. Jot down ideas *before* you write – that way, once you've started, you won't have to go back to add in points you've just remembered. Read through and check that everything's included and that you have grouped related ideas together and in logical order. Draw up a list of subjects to be covered, leaving lots of space after each so that you can add in other things as you remember them. Then subdivide each subject into the points to be covered on each. Planning is a vital stage in successful writing: once you've come up with a basic outline, it's much easier to tackle the writing itself because your thoughts have been clarified and you've broken the overall task down into smaller components.

- Number the pages in case they come apart.
- Internal memos can be simpler and shorter than letters to outside parties, where more of the courtesy padding is required.
- Try to keep the tone of any document positive.
- Avoid too many technical terms unless you're absolutely certain your reader is going to understand them. If not, make sure to clarify them.
- Explain straight away why you're writing. Don't keep it a secret from the reader until the end of the document, or you run the risk that she might give up before she gets there.
- If you're writing something that will be circulated to several different people, personalizing it by jotting a short handwritten note at the top will flatter the recipient and can be used to draw attention to a key point.
- Write the easiest bit first. Even if it comes in the middle or at the end, getting this part down will help build up your confidence. Don't feel you have to get everything perfectly phrased straight off: just bash down a rough draft, then edit it once the outline is there.
- Keep it simple, in everyday English. Pretend you're explaining your idea to a friend in a letter: it will stop you getting bogged down in business jargon or pompous over-formality and you'll get your ideas across clearly. At the same time, don't tip over into too-colloquial expressions: lots of slang and exclamation marks are not appropriate.
- Avoid clichés: they make your writing sound dull and insincere.
- If you're writing something to which someone else's name will be put – a speech for the managing director, for example – take into account their personality and write in a way that will seem natural to them.
- Make sure that you haven't made any spelling errors or grammatical gaffes: most word processors have a built-in spelling and grammar check so there's no excuse for sloppiness. A letter or memo filled with mistakes can make a terrible and lasting impression on others.
- Write as you speak. Keep it natural and you'll keep your reader's attention.

- Collect examples of well-written reports, letters and memos (your own or other people's) so that you can refer back to them for inspiration when necessary. Just getting started can be the hardest part and having past examples to look at can provide a framework to kick you off.
- Keep it short. Include only what is relevant and avoid padding with unnecessary detail. Concise is the key word. The more the reader knows about the subject, the less background explanation is needed, so make sure to keep the reader constantly in mind as you write.
- Avoid too many long words, long sentences and long paragraphs: your writing will be easier to read and your message will come across more effectively.
- Consider whether some information would be better presented in a table, graph or list form than in text: it varies the pace of the document and can make it clearer to understand.
- Use good quality paper and attractive folders – no dog-eared pages or coffee-stained cover sheets.
- Don't put anything down on paper unless you're absolutely certain of it, be it fact or opinion.
- All documents should be dated and it should be obvious to whom they are addressed and from whom they have come.
- If your document has to be read and approved by others before it can go out, double-space it, so that people have room to make any amendments.
- Bear in mind that some things may be better not put in writing. A sensitive or confidential situation should be tackled face-to-face rather than committed to paper. Also you should never put in writing anything you're not prepared to say publicly: you wouldn't be the first to be caught out by a stray memo or fax picked up by someone you'd rather didn't see it.
- If your deadlines allow, put the document aside once you've written it and come back to it the following day with a fresh eye.
- Make sure your documents look attractive, with wide margins (at least an inch either side and at the top and foot of each page) and plenty of white space, headings and subheadings to break up

big blocks of text and make it easy for a reader to understand what's going on. Put a line space between paragraphs; indent some items to make them stand out.

- If you're writing a long report, give a contents list, so that people know where to find things. Your readers are busy so everything you do to make the reading easier for them will be appreciated.
- If you have a grammatical check on your WP use it: it will alert you to any excessively long sentences, etc.
- It's usually better to phrase things in active rather than passive statements: 'We decided to' rather than 'It was decided that'. It's more immediate and therefore has more impact.
- Check through to make sure you've included all the necessary information and haven't left anything out. If you're replying to a letter or writing a report to a brief, refer back to the original to check that all the points raised have been covered. Have you presented all the information in the logical order? Have you been consistent throughout on use of spellings, style, numbering conventions, etc.?
- If you're writing a letter or memo in anger, sit on it for twenty-four hours before you send it. You may feel differently the next day and regret acting in the heat of the moment. If you do decide not to send it, don't just toss it in the bin: make sure you shred it.

Chapter 8 / **Telephone Techniques**

Most people will spend hours fine-tuning a written report or presentation yet pay little attention to how they perform on the phone. Yet it's just as important to make a good impression down the line as it is in person or on paper. And first impressions are vital – a call that lasts just a matter of seconds can give the person at the other end enough time to form a judgement of you, your company and your professional abilities.

Making Calls

- The best time to phone people is usually at the beginning of a week when they're refreshed and the end-of-week panic hasn't yet set in. Also they're usually more receptive in the morning or early afternoon. Don't call around lunchtime or right at the end of the day if you can avoid it. If you want to speak to the person for more than a few minutes, always check with them first whether or not this is a convenient time to talk and, if not, when they would prefer to speak to you later.
- Don't be rude to secretaries/PAs. If you're being palmed off with 'I'm afraid she's in a meeting' for the nth time, shouting, whining or being sarcastic isn't going to help. Just explain that you've been trying to reach the person for some time and as she's obviously extremely busy can they suggest a good time to contact her.
- Don't assume that any woman who answers a phone is a secretary.
- Always prepare before you make a call, especially if you think it's going to be a difficult one. Mentally review what you plan to

say and what you want to achieve. Have any relevant documents in front of you, plus notes if you need them.
- If you're waiting for a problem call, consider taking the initiative and making it instead. This gives you more chance to control the conversation and will surprise the person at the other end.
- Always make a note of the name of whoever you're talking to.
- Don't abuse the office phone by making too many personal calls. Most companies are sympathetic to the odd personal call but keep them brief – long-distance or long, chatty calls are right out.
- If you're in a hurry, announce at the start of the call that you have only a few minutes to talk; it will focus the other person's attention and stop you appearing rude when you have to ring off soon after.
- Don't be thrown by answering machines. Speak more slowly and clearly than normal, especially when you're giving names and numbers, and keep your message brief. Some machines automatically date and time all incoming calls but it's always a good idea to give your date and time of calling. And don't feel silly saying hello and goodbye: you may be talking to a machine, but it will be a person who listens to you.
- If you're not sure how to pronounce the name of the person you're calling, check with the switchboard first.
- When you're working through a list of calls to make, keep notes of which you've done and the outcome so that you don't get confused and call the same ones twice.

Taking Calls

- Don't answer the phone abruptly or bad-temperedly, even if it has interrupted your concentration: the person at the other end has no way of knowing whether or not they've chosen a good time to phone but will instantly pick up on your negative tone. If you don't want to be interrupted, it's better to divert your calls or leave a machine on, if possible. If not, grin and bear it when it rings but suggest to people that you call them back later when it's a better time to talk. Try to answer the phone with a smile on your face to give your voice a lift.

- Never ignore a ringing phone. In fact, you should try to answer it within three rings. If you don't have a receptionist or secretary who can take calls when you're not there, arrange for a colleague to do so and do the same for her in return. If you let the phone keep ringing, it gives an impression of inefficiency.
- Answer the phone as soon as you pick it up. Don't leave the caller listening to you finishing off your conversation: it's both rude and inefficient. Give your name or the name of your company/department when you answer.
- If you're answering someone else's phone, always find out who's calling before putting them through. If you've got a call meant for someone in another department, always try to transfer them or return them to the switchboard: if you are offhand, they may not bother calling back and you could have lost the company business. Take written messages carefully, including the date, time, caller's full name, number and nature of their call, and pass them on immediately; don't rely on your memory. If you don't catch someone's name or number first time, ask them to repeat it, then read it back to them to check you've got it right. Always try to take a number even if they're a friend or returning a call: your colleague may have mislaid their number.
- If you're going to be away from your own phone for a while, make sure you arrange for someone to answer it.
- Try to make sure that anyone else who answers your phone sounds just as professional and creates a good impression. If you're expecting a work call at home, make sure that flatmates or family know and that pen and paper are handily placed by the phone so they can take a message.
- If you have an answering machine at work, listen to your messages as frequently as possible and return the calls. Don't leave a 'fun' message – it will quickly pall. Short, simple and professional is all you need: 'We're sorry that we're unable to take your call just now. Please leave a message after the tone and we'll get back to

you as soon as possible.' Most people find computerized music on answering machines a major irritant, too.
- If you're screening calls for someone else, ask if you can help: often you will be able to deal with the query just as well as the person they asked for and the caller will be happy not to have to wait for a response.
- Develop a feel for which calls your colleagues or boss always want to be put through, and which ones are only OK if they're not too busy. If you know your boss is having a hectic day, ask which calls she considers priority and which can wait.
- If you're asking someone to hold, make sure to use the hold or secrecy button, otherwise they'll hear everything you're saying, which may not always be flattering. If you leave someone on hold for a while, come back to them periodically to check they still want to hold, otherwise they'll feel they've been forgotten.

General Phone Know-how

- Always keep pen and paper to hand by the phone so you don't have to scrabble round for them when you take a message.
- Learn how to use all the phone's features: secrecy button, last-number redial, etc.
- Remember that, in many cases, the only contact a caller will have with your company is via the telephone: any impression you make will be the impression they gain of your company as a whole, so if you are rude, offhand or vague, they'll assume the whole company is.
- Speak clearly. If someone mumbles, it's even harder to understand down a phone line than it is face-to-face. Speak directly into the mouthpiece with your mouth about an inch away from it; don't leave it hanging below your chin.
- Don't use the phone for confidential matters: arrange instead to meet in person.
- Concentrate on the call rather than trying to do two things at once, like reading papers or writing notes while you're talking. If

you don't give the caller your full attention, you may miss something important. Listen carefully and, without interrupting unnecessarily, let them know you're listening.
- Don't eat or drink while you're on the phone: it will be horribly amplified for the benefit of the person at the other end of the line.
- In the case of important conversations, be sure to take notes or record the conversation. If decisions are reached on the phone, always ask for confirmation in writing or offer to confirm details from your end. That way, you'll be sure of no misunderstanding.
- Don't leave a caller on hold without an explanation: if you have someone on the other line or have to check something and know it might take a while, offer to call them back instead – and make sure you do so promptly, even if it's to give them bad news or to let them know that it's going to take you longer than expected to find out the information. If you have to keep someone on hold, make sure you thank them for being so patient when you return to the call.
- When you're transferring someone to another person, make sure they know that's what you're doing, and explain to the person who answers that you're transferring a call to them, who it's from and briefly what it's about.
- Start each call by giving your name and/or department title. Don't assume that people will automatically recognize your voice. If you have a common first name, be sure to include your surname too.
- Sound spontaneous. If you've ever had a phone conversation with someone reading from a script (usually sales people), you'll know just how irritating and unconvincing it sounds.

Chapter 9 / **Leadership**

Once you reach management level, you must learn how to lead and motivate other people, which can be hard when you have been conditioned to work for others rather than asking them to work for you. When you first take up a management role it can be difficult to know just how to play it. Do you go for the friendly and approachable tactic and risk the staff looking on you as a weak person with no authority? Or do you decide to let people know straight away who's in charge and distance yourself overnight from your peers?

Leadership isn't just about giving orders. It's about getting the best from other people, involving, interesting and inspiring them. You have to know how to motivate your staff, how to make decisions, how to delegate effectively, how to gain others' respect and project a professional image, how to get people working together as a team. But don't worry if you find that prospect daunting: good leaders are rarely born but learn through experience.

Motivating Staff

- Make people feel valued by taking an interest in them, their work and their interests. You should know everybody's names (and use them), titles and what their job involves. People who feel well treated will give far more to the job than those who feel overlooked or neglected.
- Be visible and approachable and listen to what your staff have to say. As well as leading, you have to provide support. Let them know when you're available for them to discuss problems, give feedback, etc.

- It's important to ensure that your staff have a full understanding of the contribution they make to the department, and what role the department plays in the organization as a whole. Good communication is crucial to getting the results you want, so never assume that people will know what you're after – tell them. They need to be clear about what their duties and responsibilities are and what targets and performance levels you expect them to achieve.
- Have regular appraisals with them, to go through their job description and check that it is still relevant. This should be at least every six months. Discuss any problems and set objectives.
- Allocate work so that it makes the best possible use of each person's skills, interests and abilities. People who are doing jobs below or beyond their ability will not perform well and will become fed up and frustrated.
- When appointing new members of staff, don't look at them in isolation but consider how they will fit into the team, how their skills complement those of existing staff, etc.
- If you have to go away for any length of time, make sure that everyone knows who they should report to in your absence.
- Be friendly to your staff but without overstepping the mark and getting too close – you have to ensure that they still treat you as a leader and that can be hard to do unless you maintain a certain distance.
- Give your staff regular feedback on their performance and always remember to praise people when they have done something well. Acknowledge it not only to them but in front of others, giving credit where credit is due. Positive feedback encourages.
- Be aware of people's differences – in ability, attitude, ways of working.
- Know your job: you can't expect respect from your staff if you don't know how to do it properly.
- Always stay calm and keep your cool. If you panic, it will infect the rest of the staff and you should be supporting them. When pressure hits, you have to show that you can take it.
- Get people involved. Encourage ideas and input from team

members and, where possible, give them the responsibility for putting them into action.

- Be aware of others' insecurities. When changes are made to the way in which your department works, make sure that everyone is kept fully informed of what is going on at all stages. Many people are resistant to change because they fear they may lose their job or colleagues or be unable to cope – but their anxiety will be reduced if they realize that you are aware of how the changes will affect them and have taken that into account.
- Do not interfere constantly with your subordinates' work.
- Take responsibility for the working conditions of your staff and make sure they have the best possible physical environment in which to work. Speak up for them when necessary.
- You have to set an example. Work at least as hard as your team and don't ask them to put in more than you're prepared to put in yourself. Most people don't mind working overtime now and then, for instance, but they'll be resentful if it's always them who does it while the boss swans off at five o'clock every night.
- Develop your staff by recommending and providing training where appropriate, both to improve their efficiency in their current job and to prepare them for promotion.
- Once you're in a new role, don't make the mistake of hanging on to too many tasks from your previous job. Learn to delegate tasks and authority (see chapter 14 for hints) and focus on your new responsibilities instead.
- Remember that people make judgements based on appearance: if you want to be treated as the boss, make sure you look the part.
- Set a positive example by being encouraging, enthusiastic and optimistic. You are a role model for your staff and enthusiasm from you will encourage it in them. Apathy and a negative attitude are contagious and destructive. Be loyal about the company.
- Be seen to not pass the buck and to take responsibility for your own actions.
- It's only natural that you will like some members of staff more than others but try to treat everyone equally, with no obvious signs

of favouritism or dislike. Everyone should be subject to the same standards of time-keeping and discipline.
- Respect other people's abilities, however junior their job.
- The different people within your team should also understand what the other team members do and what contribution they make.
- Accept that you won't always be popular: people won't always like your decisions but you must accept that you can't please everybody all the time. It's their respect you need to gain more than their affection and if people think you are desperate to be liked they will see you as a soft touch. Ultimately you're employed to get the job done, and done on time, not to make friends.
- If you're moving into your first leadership or management role, ask the company if they can send you on any training courses that will help you to handle the new challenges.
- If you're promoted over people who used to be your peers it can be particularly difficult, especially if some applied for the same job. You have to make it clear that you're not about to become a power-mad monster and that, while you expect them to acknowledge your new position, you also need their help and support. Tell them as soon as you know about the promotion rather than letting them find out from someone else. Don't apologize or run yourself down – assume that if they are your friends, they'll be happy for you. Remember that you got the job because you were the best person for it and you deserve to be where you are.
- Don't rush in and start making changes straight away. Take time to get to know the lie of the land otherwise you'll alienate people. If others are feeling insecure about the effect you, as a new boss, will have on their job, make it clear that as far as you're concerned, you're all working on the same side and they shouldn't see you as a threat. Any changes you may eventually want to make will only be after careful consideration and consultation.
- One of the main responsibilities of a leader is discipline. It is down to you to ensure that the department functions efficiently, and if someone is letting the side down, you must take whatever action is necessary – and don't feel guilty about it. You must set the

rules, make sure everyone is clear what they are and see that they stick to them. If somebody doesn't, they must be brought back in line. See chapter 16 for tips on behaving assertively.

• If you need to discipline someone, do it in private. Tearing a strip off them in front of the whole office is the kind of thing they might never forgive you for, and you'll end up with sulky, resentful staff. Try to phrase any criticism positively, suggesting solutions rather than just stating problems. Don't be apologetic about it, though: if someone isn't coming up to scratch, it's part of your job to let them know about it and not something you should feel guilty about. Look them in the eye when you're addressing them so you make more of an impact. Let the other person put their side of the story too, then work together to resolve the problem. Don't harp on past mistakes. Make sure you know what your company's disciplinary and grievance procedures are.

• Always be honest: trust, once lost, is almost impossible to regain, but if people know they can always believe you, you'll have their respect.

Decision-making

• Be decisive: few things are more frustrating than trying to work for a boss who doesn't know what she wants. Sometimes staff would rather you made a decision they disagreed with than dithered, not knowing what you want. Vagueness suggests a lack of confidence in yourself, which doesn't inspire others to have confidence in you.

• Not every decision you make will be the right one, but as long as you learn from it, it won't necessarily be a total disaster.

• Never take decisions above your level of authority. If you need to involve or consult other people, do so. If others have more experience and ideas on a subject, ask their opinion. If your decision will affect others, get their input too.

• Weigh up the risks and consequences of each decision. What will happen if you get it wrong? List the pros and cons on paper.

- Pay attention to all your thoughts: if you have a nagging doubt, don't ignore it – think it through.
- Avoid making on-the-spot decisions, if possible: it's usually better to take time to consider your options.
- If you make the wrong decision, own up to it. Everyone makes mistakes and you'll earn more respect by admitting yours than you will by trying to cover up or pass the buck.
- Whenever you make a decision, explain the reasons behind it: people are more likely to accept it and co-operate when they know why it was reached.

Chapter 10 / **How to Manage Meetings**

How do you feel after an office meeting? Pleased with your contribution, satisfied that the meeting was worthwhile and fired with new enthusiasm and ideas? Or are you more likely to feel frustrated and aware that you've just wasted several precious hours of work time?

Daunting though they may be, meetings can be the perfect chance to show colleagues how well you perform. Unfair as it may seem, the impression you make here could carry far more weight than your everyday work, especially if this is the only time you come into contact with more senior staff – people who can influence your pay and promotion prospects. They're far more likely to notice a person who stands out in a one-off meeting than an equally worthy worker who keeps her head down and does her job well but never speaks up.

If you have meetings with people outside your own company, this can also be a good chance to broaden your contacts and impress other people in your field of work, which could be useful when you're looking for another job.

How to Shine

- Always prepare ahead. Make sure you know what's on the agenda so you can think through what you want to say and gather any necessary information to back you up. Anticipate queries and objections and have your answers ready. Read any papers distributed beforehand so you don't waste time doing it at the meeting or look a fool by showing your ignorance. Try to find out who else will be attending and what their role/interests are.

- Arrive promptly – forget that one last phone call or quick letter. Being late will make you look inefficient and disorganized, give you less choice of seat and may cause you to miss out on important discussion.
- Make sure you say something, however much the thought may terrify you. It can be hard to break in but the earlier you do it the better – it gets harder the longer you leave it.
- Always take pen and paper with you, a copy of the agenda, if there is one and any papers relevant to the meeting.
- Listen to what others have to say rather than rehearsing your own points.
- Don't be intimidated by others: there's no such thing as a right or a wrong point of view, just different but equally valid opinions. If others disagree with some of the things you say, don't take it personally: it's the idea they're rejecting, not you, and no one's ideas are accepted all the time.
- Don't feel you have to make a long, involved speech: short, sharp comments are just as effective.
- Keep to the point: nothing is more annoying in a meeting than people who persist in wandering off the point and sidetracking everybody into discussing irrelevant issues. If there is something you think should be discussed, suggest it be added to the agenda for the next meeting, or propose that a separate meeting be arranged.
- Make your points when it's appropriate to make them, rather than pitching them in as they come to mind. The timing of your contributions can be as important as their content.
- Control your voice: pitch it low and talk more slowly and slightly louder than normal. Look up at other people rather than down at your notes: your voice will carry better and command more attention. Try to speak fluently, avoiding irritating mumbling or hesitation.
- If you have opinions on several subjects, bring them in one point at a time, rather than trying to cover everything in one go. And don't repeat yourself.
- Don't interrupt – or allow others to interrupt you. If someone

cuts in while you're talking, point out firmly that you have a few more brief comments you'd like to make.
- Stay positive and steer clear of putting yourself down by prefacing your contributions with comments like 'You probably won't agree with this, but . . .' or 'This may sound a bit stupid but . . .' Why destroy your own credibility?
- Watch where you sit. Try to be somewhere where most people can see you and you can easily attract their attention when you wish to speak.
- Remember your manners: arrive on time, don't whisper to the person sitting next to you and don't show you're bored by slumping and doodling.
- Keep an open mind. Put your personal dislikes to one side and stay receptive to others' ideas.
- Don't attempt to impress with convoluted sentences or technical jargon: pompous language will simply bore and alienate everyone else.
- If you disagree with someone, don't be too critical: think how you'd feel in their place if someone shot you down in flames. Concentrate on the positive and keep your comments constructive: then you'll make allies instead of enemies.
- If you're the only woman there and someone asks you to pour the tea or take minutes, don't make a fuss but don't do it. If they persist, don't back down: calmly, but firmly, repeat your original refusal until they realize you're not going to give in.
- If you have regular routine meetings at which little is ever achieved, suggest that the format might be changed to revive them – for example, different people could be invited, the meetings could be held less frequently, different people could take turns to chair, etc.
- Meetings can eat up a lot of time so before you attend one, make sure first of all that you really need to be there.
- If you have a major problem that you know will prey on your mind and distract you just when you're supposed to be paying attention, try to reschedule the meeting for later in the week or at a time when you will be less preoccupied.

When You're in the Chair

The chair has the task of organizing and controlling a meeting. This includes planning and preparation before the meeting as well as chairing it.
- First decide whether it's necessary to have a meeting. If the aim is to reach a decision, consult on problem-solving, etc., then fine. But if it is simply to relay information, could it be better done by memo, e-mail, etc.?
- Decide who to invite and keep numbers down as much as possible: the larger the meeting, the longer it usually lasts. Make sure that only the necessary people are there: about six is the maximum for a good working number. Shyer people might be intimidated by a large group.
- Draw up an agenda, to give a structure to the meeting and focus attention on the key issues. Try not to cram in too much and have an idea of how much time to allow for each item. Begin with simple things (announcements, easy discussions, etc.) to warm people up before getting into the main, more important and perhaps difficult topics. Wind down with easier items at the end.
- Make sure before the meeting that everybody knows when and where it will take place, who will be attending, what is to be discussed and what the goal of the meeting is. Circulate any documents people need to read in advance and let them know they are expected to do so. This should be done no less than a week ahead so that they have time to prepare. Tell them if there is any specific information they'll be asked for or any documents they should bring with them, etc.
- Check that the venue is suitable – not too cold or too hot, big enough for everyone, enough chairs, provided with any facilities or visual aids that will be needed.
- Reiterate the goal at the start of the meeting and introduce any outsiders (rehearse this in advance if it helps).
- The chairperson's behaviour and attitude has a big effect on

that of the other participants. If you're enthusiastic and interested, that will give a positive feel; if you're bored, they'll pick up on that too. It's important that you appear confident and in control.
- Try to make sure that everyone contributes. Draw out shy people by asking questions, but don't pick only on them or they'll be terrified – ask for their input on a point that you know they have experience or knowledge of. Rein back the over-talkers.
- You need to sit in a central position where you can see and be seen by everyone else. Consider other people's seating arrangements, too: if possible, it's probably best to keep rivals apart from each other.
- Try to keep the mood light – you don't have to crack jokes every few minutes but a bit of humour puts people at ease and helps them to open up.
- Discourage interruptions from outside and let everybody know that they are expected to arrive on time and stay until the end.
- Make sure everyone sticks to the subject in hand and summarize occasionally so that they know where they are. Keep notes of the key points as you go along. Keep things on track, explaining at the start of the meeting why you're there and how long you think it should take, and roughly how long you plan to devote to each item on the agenda.
- As well as ensuring that the meeting runs to time, you must also encourage the flow of discussion and creative input: be sensitive to when people need reining in and when the brainstorming is leading somewhere.
- You may have to take the deciding vote on any points of action so be attentive and receptive throughout.
- Be polite, respectful and impartial towards all members. You mustn't let personal prejudice and office politics get in your way – and take steps to check them in others.
- At the end, summarize what has been decided and make sure everyone knows what action, if any, they are expected to take.
- After the meeting, ensure that minutes, summarizing the main points of the meeting, are circulated quickly.

Chapter 11 / **Time Management**

When there don't seem to be enough hours in the day to do everything you've got to do, it's time to work smarter, not harder, with these time-management techniques.

- Watch other people for ideas of ways in which they save time.
- Learn to say no: you may be having problems fitting in all your work because there really is too much of it. Speak up: make sure your department head knows the situation. Battling on against the odds is a waste of your time and energy, but a cry for help usually brings a positive response.
- Jot handwritten replies on memos and return them rather than taking time to compose a proper reply. When it comes to paperwork, bin it, file it, delegate it or act on it – now.
- Don't be too perfectionist. While every task should be done to the best of your ability, there are days when getting everything just so can take up too much time. Better for the minutes of a meeting to be circulated the week after a meeting than to hang on to them for another fortnight while you agonize over just the right phrasing.
- Learn to think ahead rather than concentrating solely on the daily tasks – that way you can anticipate problems.
- Try to plan your work and update it regularly. Bear in mind that, however well you plan, there will always be some unexpected interruptions, but if the routine work is under control, the interruptions won't come as such a blow. Whatever happens, don't panic: think things through coolly and rationally.
- If you don't manage your time properly, you'll be inefficient and seen to be inefficient.
- Poor time management on your part has a knock-on effect on other members of staff, holding up their work and therefore costing the company time and money.

- The more you try to rush things, the more likely you are to make a mess of them.
- If the same crises keep occurring, investigate ways to avert them.
- Try to give yourself deadlines for completing each piece of work: if you have something to work towards, you're more likely to meet it.
- Learn to use your computer properly: if you know all the short-cuts and time-saving tricks, it can cut precious minutes off your work. If necessary, ask the company for refresher training or get someone in the computer-support department to give you half an hour's training. If you do a lot of work on screen, learning to type properly will also save you time. Most colleges offer flexible touch-typing courses.
- Speed-reading courses can also be a help if you have lots of paperwork to deal with. Learn to skim things rapidly to get an overview when it's not necessary to read in depth. Could you get someone else to screen your post and bin all the irrelevant stuff before it gets to you? If you regularly receive mail or magazines that are of no use to you, get your name taken off the mailing list or ensure that they are sent to someone else.
- Tackle the most important tasks at the time when you know you're at your best: if your mental peak is mid-morning, save demanding work till then; if you don't get going till after lunch, ditto.
- Try to identify where your time is going at the moment and keep a rough diary for a typical week, noting approximate times spent on different activities such as taking calls, being in meetings, visiting clients, etc. Make a real effort not to forget or distort.
- While the odd missed lunch hour or late night won't hurt you, don't make a habit of it. You need to take time out from work or you'll burn out: sometimes the lunch hour could be much more profitably spent with a friend relaxing and forgetting work than sitting resentfully and wearily at your desk.
- Take stock regularly of how your work is going and reassess your workload, commitments and deadlines every week. Try to

start every week uncluttered and organized, if necessary setting aside Friday afternoons for admin and clearing up.
- Remember that things nearly always take longer than expected and allow for that when you're setting deadlines. Then if you finish early you can give people a pleasant surprise.
- Keep your workplace tidy so that you don't waste precious minutes hunting for things on a messy desk. (According to one survey, the average office worker spends around seventeen days a year searching for lost paperwork.) Have regular clear-outs and don't hang on to too much paper.
- Keep a to-do list and tick off items as they're done: it ensures things don't get forgotten and gives you a great feeling of satisfaction as you cross them off.
- Try to touch each piece of paper only once: when you read a letter make your decision and act on it straight away rather than half reading it then putting it aside to come back to later.
- Make outgoing telephone calls in a batch.

How to Stop Others Wasting Your Time

However well you may schedule your own time and however organized you are, other people's behaviour is harder to control. Open-plan offices can be especially distracting: people are far more likely to interrupt if they're sitting opposite you, whereas they might think twice if they have to get up and walk to another office.

Women are especially bad at saying no or turning away people who are making demands on them. But there *are* ways of dealing with time-wasters at work.
- If you're lucky enough to have your own office, the way you arrange the furniture can help. If you don't want people to sit down, don't have a spare chair, or, if you have one, leave papers and books on it. Position your desk so that people walking by can't just catch your eye but have to enter properly: this will deter casual callers. You may normally prefer to leave the door open, allowing

people to drop in, but if necessary, shut it and put up a notice making it quite clear that you don't want to be interrupted until whatever time you will be free again if someone needs to see you.
- Never believe anyone who says something will only take a minute of your time. It's hardly ever true.
- If someone wants to talk about a matter that needs discussing properly, explain that you don't have time to give it the attention it deserves right now but you'll be happy to go through it with them later – and fix a time to do so. Far from being offended, they may feel flattered that you're taking their work so seriously.
- Freelances and home-workers can be especially bothered by others who think that because they're at home they're available at all times of day. Make it clear to friends and neighbours that during work hours your home should be treated like any other place of work. After all, they wouldn't drop in for a cup of tea if you worked in an office.
- In emergencies, find a quiet room at the office (maybe a sick room or unoccupied meeting room) to hide yourself away – but make sure *someone* knows where you are in case something urgent comes up, and arrange for someone to answer your calls.
- If you're in charge of meetings, try to avoid inviting people you know will waffle on, or impress upon them in advance that time will be tight and they must prepare their arguments as concisely as possible. If meetings regularly overrun, try scheduling them for late in the day, maybe even on a Friday afternoon, which might inspire people to finish on time.
- Meetings can be a major time-waster, and the bigger they are, the longer they take. If your working life seems to be one long round of meetings, try to cut them back. Never agree to attend one without checking first whether or not you really need to be there. If you don't, delegate attendance.
- A constantly ringing telephone is one of the most irritating of interruptions – but if you won't allow colleagues to disturb you in person, why should you let the phone destroy your train of thought? Try to arrange for someone else to take your calls: you

may not have your own secretary but colleagues may be prepared to help, especially if you promise to return the favour in *their* hour of need.
- If you *are* interrupted by a phone call, don't let your voice betray your irritation. A person approaching your desk may see how busy you are and understand but someone at the other end of a phone line has no visual clues and will just mark you down as bad-tempered. Simply explain that this is a difficult time to talk and promise to call back later when you can give the conversation your full attention – and do so.
- Discourage colleagues who persistently chatter about personal matters during work hours. If a colleague keeps discussing her social life when you're trying to work, tell her you really are busy at the moment, but you'd love to hear about it over lunch or during a coffee break. Of course we all want to be friends with workmates but the bottom line is that your employer is paying you to carry out your job and that should come first.
- Remember that not all chit-chat is time-wasting. In creative environments, especially, chatting can produce ideas – and you need some light relief in the day.
- Try to do work that requires full concentration at quiet times of the day when interruptions won't be so frequent: coming in an hour earlier in the morning allows you to get plenty done before colleagues arrive to disturb you. Or, if necessary, ask your boss if you could work from home for a day, or even outside normal working hours in return for a day off during the week. If you'd be too easily distracted at home, try the local library.
- Don't waste time dealing with things someone else could handle. If a matter could be dealt with by a subordinate, delegate it. (See chapter 14 for tips on how to delegate.)
- If you know in advance that a certain visitor is likely to take up too much of your time, arrange for someone to interrupt at an appointed hour to say, for example, that your next appointment is waiting, there's an urgent call from New York on the other line or a taxi has arrived to take you somewhere else.
- The right body language could save you having to say anything.

When you want to signal that a conversation is over, lean forward in your seat as if to get up, gather up your papers or stand and start moving towards the door. At the same time, don't go too far: avoid making people uncomfortable with obvious signs of impatience such as drumming fingers or tapping feet, and although most people will take the hint if you glance at your clock or watch they may leave feeling miffed.

- Going to see someone instead of letting them come to you means that *you* can decide when to leave.
- Make use of new technology. If you can send messages on a computer system, people will be encouraged to answer in the same way, which is much quicker than dealing with them face-to-face.
- Put aside a regular time each day for staff to come to you: if they know they will definitely have a chance to talk to you at a certain time, they're less likely to come looking for you in the meantime.
- Be flexible: some interruptions are important. Don't make people so wary of disturbing you that they let something urgent go unattended or can't get on with things.

Chapter 12 / **How to Organize and Prioritize**

Some days everything seems to go haywire. You're up to your eyes in work, the phones keep ringing – then along comes the boss with another urgent task. Where on earth do you start? The important skill in these situations is knowing how to decide what's most important. Sounds simple – but it's surprising how many people seem unable to do this and start to panic instead. That, in turn, leads to unnecessary stress. If you can sort out your priorities, you're well on the way to keeping your work under control. And the knock-on effect of that is that you'll be seen as efficient because you won't be caught unawares or asked for work you haven't completed.

Like every other skill, learning to prioritize may seem difficult at first but keep practising. In the end it will make your working life a whole lot easier.

Assess Your Workload

- Don't wait for panic to set in before you start trying to sort yourself out. Get into the habit of organizing your priorities all the time and set yourself goals and deadlines on a regular basis.
- If your boss gives you three things to do, all urgent, *ask* which is the most important. Ask for a specific deadline, too. One person's 'urgent' or 'as soon as possible' may mean by the end of the week; to another, it could mean within the hour. You can't know without asking, so always check – and be specific in the deadlines you give others too.

- Make a things-to-do list daily, either on a notepad or on your computer. Update it every morning and refer back to it throughout the day.
- Learn to recognize the people who call *everything* urgent as a matter of course. It may make *their* job easier if you do your bit faster, but remember to balance that against how hard it makes *your* job.
- If someone persistently passes work on to you at the last minute because they can't organize their *own* workload efficiently, *say* something. Point out to them that they're making your work difficult and you'd appreciate it if they could think ahead more. Obviously, you should be tactful.
- You can't carry on being overworked indefinitely so let people know if you're ridiculously overloaded. If your boss is making unreasonable demands, talk to her about it. Avoid moaning when explaining the situation: people don't react well to a whining voice. Simply explain clearly and coolly how overloaded you are and why.
- When you know you won't be able to complete an important task on time, tell your boss immediately.
- When you genuinely have too much to do, speak to your boss about the possibility of getting temporary staff in to help out over the busy period. Work out how long you would need someone for, and explain the possible consequences if you don't have any assistance.

Organize Your Time

- Be rational. When every task seems urgent, look at each in turn and ask yourself what would happen if you didn't do it today. Thinking of the consequences will help you work out which is the right job to concentrate on. Would a delay cost the company a lot of money? Is someone else putting unnecessary pressure on you to do something because they haven't got their own priorities sorted out?

- What *must* be done? What *should* be done? What would you *like* to do? Setting priorities means deciding what you *need* to do next; it's not a question of what you *feel* like doing. Divide work into 'must' and 'want' categories and tackle them in that order.
- Don't procrastinate. We sometimes tend to work on minor tasks while something bigger – and tougher – is lurking in the background. Urgent jobs are not always fun but the longer you leave them the harder they get. An irate customer waiting for you to return their call will become even more irate the longer they have to wait. Bite the bullet and do any unpleasant tasks as quickly as possible: they'll never be fun but at least they won't be hanging over your head, spoiling your ability to concentrate on the rest of your work.
- If you find yourself in a situation where you have half a dozen things to do that are genuinely and equally urgent, try to delegate but do it wisely. It's no use delegating an important task to someone who's not up to it; if you do, you run the risk of things going wrong and bouncing back on you to sort out – when time is even tighter.
- If several things are 'pending', waiting on feedback from others, make sure to remind those involved that they are holding up your work.

Minimize the Pressure

- Take only urgent calls. If possible, get a secretary to screen your calls at busy times so that you're not constantly disturbed. An answerphone is another option. If it's an emergency and you don't have a secretary, ask a colleague to do it for you with the promise that you'll return the favour another time – and make sure you do! Don't make a habit of this, though, or the helper will become resentful and feel taken for granted.
- In the same way, colleagues may be willing to help out in really busy times, as long as they know they can rely on you to help them

in their hour of need. Don't abuse people's goodwill or you'll find they won't be so happy to chip in next time.
- Meetings are time-consuming so if you're working on an urgent matter and a non-essential meeting is scheduled, see either if it can be postponed or if someone else could attend in your place. But don't make a habit of it or others will see you as unreliable. If you have meetings outside your office that will involve time wasted in travel, try to relocate them to your home ground.
- If you have to travel, going by train will allow you to get some work done. The car won't.
- If one of your urgent tasks involves liaising with other people to arrange something, make contact with those people first, then get on with the work you can do on your own. That way, if anyone is away or out, you can make alternative arrangements, not be left panicking at the last moment.
- It isn't always best – or possible – to complete each area of work before moving on to another so break large tasks down into smaller chunks. For example, start the ball rolling on one project by putting in a few phone calls, then, while you wait for results, continue your research for next week's meeting before putting the finishing touches to that report you wrote a few days ago. It often helps to come back to a subject at intervals, with a fresh eye, rather than getting bogged down in it by trying to do it all at once.
- You're doing nobody any favours if you always take on all the work that's handed to you, however overloaded you are, without explaining when it's hard for you to cope. If things go wrong, as they well may, other people could be justifiably aggrieved that you didn't tell them *beforehand* that it would be a problem to do the work on time.
- Make sure people know when they can't interrupt you. If they drop by your desk for a quick chat, tell them it's a bad time and you'll speak to them later. Don't moan about how pressed you are, yet still sit there chattering.
- Develop a filing system that works for you and set aside some

time every week to do filing and other routine chores – things that are easier kept under regular contol. Be selective about what you keep – 85 per cent of all filed material is never looked at again, so don't feel you have to hang on to every single sheet of paper 'just in case'.
• Record notes and important phone conversations in a hardback notebook rather than on odd sheets of paper or Post-Its, which are easily lost.
• If you regularly receive letters and information from companies that are of no interest to you, ask to be taken off their mailing list. If relevant, pass them on to someone else in the organization who might be interested to hear from them.

Your Personal Priorities

• Prioritizing isn't just about work: your personal life is important too. Health should always be high priority, whatever the situation at work – in fact, the busier you are, the more important it is to pay attention to your physical well-being. Without that, everything else falls apart, so make sure that you eat well and take rest breaks when you can.
• Use whatever techniques work for you to ensure that at the end of the working day, you can switch off and relax. If you stay mentally bogged down in work problems, they will invade your dreams and spoil your sleep.
• Keep a positive frame of mind: humour and grace under pressure are vital if you're to appear professional.
• Be flexible. Priorities can never be cast-iron: urgent, last-minute things will always turn up so you have to be ready to shuffle your workload around to accommodate them. Accept that occasionally you will have to work late or maybe even at weekends to catch up. However, this should *not* be the norm.

Avoiding Holiday Hassle

All too often the mountains of messages, unopened post and piles of work that greet you on your return from holiday can make you wonder if it was worth going away, but you can make things easier for yourself by preparing properly before you go.

- Leave clear instructions with any colleagues who'll be handling your work while you're away: don't expect them to know what to do. Write down full details, even the things that seem glaringly obvious.
- Let them know if you're expecting anything particular to crop up in your absence and how to deal with it.
- Make sure customers and colleagues know who will replace you in the event of a crisis: it's infuriating to ring someone with an urgent request only to find that they're on holiday and your problem can't be dealt with until they return in two weeks' time.
- If you can, arrange for a colleague to open your post while you're away and sort it out into categories (memos, letters, projects, etc.). It will make your desk less disorganized and more welcoming when you come back – and you can return the favour later on.
- If you're really worried that things might fall apart in your absence, leave a number where the office can reach you. Bear in mind that they might abuse this and stress in no uncertain terms that it's for use only in the direst of emergencies. That way, you can relax in the certainty that if the phone doesn't ring they're coping without you.

Chapter 13 / **Negotiation**

You may associate negotiation with arms deals and union–management talks, but it's more common than that. It's what we do whenever we try to work things out with someone: asking the boss for a rise, for example, or bargaining for an extended deadline.

The idea in successful negotiation is to reach mutual agreement, and for each side to get something of importance to them in exchange for something they consider less important. They may not get all they want, but they should have enough to feel satisfied.

Before You Meet

Successful negotiation comes as a result of careful planning.
- Assess your position and define your goals. Be clear about: what you *want* to achieve; what you *need* and would settle for; and what you're prepared to give up to get what you want or need.
- Remember that price alone isn't the only negotiable: you can also do deals on dates, interest rates, quantities, qualities, deadlines, etc.
- Look at things from the other party's side, too. Try to anticipate all potential objections so you can prepare the answers in advance.
- Find out all you can about the person/company you're negotiating with. The more you know about them and what they want from the negotiations, the better equipped you are.
- Prepare your case and your strategy for presenting it to the other party.
- Stay flexible and have alternative solutions and approaches ready – it's hard for the other side to say no to *everything*.

- Make sure you've done your background research. Gather information to support every point you make. The more back-up knowledge you have, the more confident you'll be and the better you'll cope with the unexpected.
- Make sure you're negotiating with the right person, someone who has the authority to take decisions, otherwise you're just wasting time.
- Consider the knock-on effect of any concessions and be sure it won't be adverse.
- Remember that the idea is to get something of value to you in exchange for something you consider to be of less value.
- Memorize what you want to say. If there are specific figures or quotes you might forget, jot them down on cards.
- Be realistic, but don't aim too low. People who enter negotiations with high expectations usually get a better deal than those with low ones.
- The hallmarks of a good negotiator are: sensitivity to the needs of other people; patience; good listening and communication skills; willingness to compromise; high tolerance for stress and conflict.

In Negotiations

- Meet on your own territory if possible – it gives you the edge.
- However nervous you feel, try to look and sound confident. Let the other person realize that you are knowledgeable on the subject.
- Dress smartly. You'll feel more confident and won't have to fight prejudice against the way you look.
- Try to get the other side to kick off: it helps you to calculate your starting point and gauge the mood.
- Don't rush straight into hard bargaining. Take time to size up the opposition and get to know them a bit.
- Don't promise more than you can deliver and don't promise

anything at all if you don't have the authority to do so (although if that's the case, you shouldn't be negotiating in the first place).
- Being justified in asking for something doesn't mean you'll get it: how you ask is vital. Don't demand, beg or threaten. If you demand and get what you want, the other party feels defeated – you may win this time round, but it creates bad feeling which could affect future negotiations.
- Watch for give-away body language from the other side and keep a check on your own: you don't want to let them know if you feel worried or uncomfortable.
- Be assertive, not aggressive; persuasive, not intimidating: bullying only leads to defensiveness.
- Don't put all your cards on the table at once; hold something in reserve in case things get stuck.
- Be persistent: don't give up at the first sign of things not going your way. If necessary, retire to reconsider and arrange to meet again at a later date.
- Stay cool. When you lose your temper, you lose control.
- In negotiations covering several issues, try to reach agreement on each point as you go along, rather than finalizing everything together. It helps in building up a positive atmosphere.
- Don't be greedy. You're unlikely to get *all* you want – just try for as much as possible while remembering that negotiation isn't a test of power, and compromise isn't a sign of failure. Keep looking for common ground.
- Listen carefully to what the other party has to say (see chapter 6 for hints on how to be a good listener). Watch for statements beginning, 'What if . . . ?', 'Supposing . . .' or 'How about . . .' as a sign that the other side may be moving towards compromise.
- When an agreement is reached, summarize discussions and make sure all are clear on what has been agreed. Get written confirmation as soon as possible.
- Practise your negotiating abilities whenever possible; whether it's haggling for jewellery on holiday or asking shopkeepers if they'll give you a discount for cash, the same principles apply. The more you do it, the more confident you'll become.

- Remember that everything is negotiable, although it may not always seem like it at first.
- Don't be afraid to ask. You'll never know what you could have had if you don't try.

Chapter 14 / **Delegation**

You don't have to be a high-flyer to delegate. All effective managers do it, and if you want to be promoted you need to learn this skill. The idea of delegation sounds enviably easy: you may think that it's just a question of picking out the bits you don't like and passing them on to someone else. Well, no, it isn't that simple. Delegation involves an element of risk and there's a definite skill involved in deciding what to delegate, when and to whom. You need to be careful to delegate without arousing resentments. And if you're used to doing the work yourself, it can be tricky to make the mental adjustment to asking other people to do it for you.

When to Delegate

- Constant overwork can make you inefficient, so it's in everyone's interests for you to recognize that the time has come to delegate. Make a list of all your current duties. What tasks could you safely pass on to someone else? Delegate the jobs that you feel confident can be easily handled by someone else to free you to concentrate on the ones that either can't or shouldn't be.
- You may feel it's simpler to do a job yourself than to tell someone else how to do it but although it takes time and patience to explain a task that you could do without thinking, the hours you spend in training now will save you many more in the future. See it as a long-term investment.
- If you're not sure that you have the authority to delegate, ask your boss.
- As you move up and acquire new responsibilities, you must learn to relinquish old ones. Don't fill your day with familiar

routine to avoid tackling new tasks about which you may not feel so confident. We often don't want to pass on work that we can do precisely because we *can* do it and like to feel in control. But part of moving up is taking on new challenges and mastering them – and the higher you climb, the more important it is for you to be involved in future planning for the company rather than day-to-day work. Delegation helps colleagues fulfil their potential and works for *you*, too, freeing you for new tasks.

• Perfectionism can often stop people delegating: they're convinced no one else could do the job as well as them. Most tasks can be delegated, though, and you may even find that a fresh eye will see new, possibly even better, ways of dealing with the work.

• Delegation is an essential part of a manager's job, freeing you for the more strategic management/planning work you're employed to do: it doesn't mean you're not up to your job or that you're exploiting others.

What to Delegate

• Don't delegate anything that a senior colleague has specifically asked you to be in charge of, a task that requires a large measure of judgement and decision-making, or anything that is strictly confidential.

• Don't pass on only the mundane, routine tasks; delegate some interesting ones as well. That said, try to assess your work objectively; jobs that you find boring, perhaps because you've been doing them for a while, may seem fresh and challenging to someone else.

• Unless you have a PA specially employed to cosset you, don't delegate non-work-related tasks. Asking someone to collect your dry cleaning or to shop for your dinner party will almost certainly cause resentment. Very few people are genuinely *so* busy that they can't take care of their own personal matters.

How to Delegate

- If you have the authority to delegate, then delegate with authority! Don't ask people to perform tasks as though they're doing you a huge favour. They may think they *are* doing you a favour and feel resentful rather than viewing new areas of work as natural career progression.
- Be aware of your subordinates and the progress they're making. Only delegate a major task if you feel the person is ready to take on more responsibility and is confident they can do it (if they're not confident of their abilities but you are, then some morale-boosting is called for). Encourage people who show an interest but don't be bullied into delegating to somebody who's not ready for more responsibility.
- Delegate the appropriate authority as well as the work itself; the person doing the task shouldn't have to keep running back to you. Tell them which areas you *must* be consulted on and which areas they can handle alone, so they know how much freedom they have; equally, make it clear that they can refer back to you on *anything* if they feel unsure.
- Be realistic about time: if you've been aware for weeks of something that needs doing, no one will appreciate your dumping a task on them a few days before the deadline.
- Brief clearly and fully: you can't expect someone to perform well if they don't understand the task. Let them know exactly *what* is needed and by *when*. If you know of any potential problems, make sure they know about them, too, so that they can prepare for them.
- Let other people know what you've delegated and to whom so they can take their queries to the right person.
- Make sure that you're not delegating to someone who is already overloaded and therefore simply transferring the problem to them.
- Effective delegation creates more capable staff, so you can be

more confident, for example, about taking time off for holidays, knowing that people can cope in your absence.

Giving Feedback

- Without constantly looking over people's shoulders, make sure to keep an eye on work you've delegated. Arrange a weekly meeting for a progress update or make a point of asking now and then what's happening. Monitor more closely in the beginning, less closely as their ability (and your confidence) grows. It's a balancing act: too much checking up will be interpreted as interference; too little may leave subordinates unclear as to whether what they are doing is right or not.
- Different doesn't mean wrong and your approach isn't the only one. No two people will tackle a task in exactly the same way, so don't fret if a subordinate handles a matter differently from the way you would: it's the end result that's important. Unless things are obviously heading towards disaster, wait for results before you criticize.
- One frequently heard complaint about senior staff is that they take all the credit for work done by their subordinates. If a junior performs well, it reflects on you and highlights your management skills so don't be afraid to give recognition and credit where it's due.
- Give feedback on delegated tasks as soon as possible. Let people know how well they're doing (or what they've done wrong); don't assume they'll know without being told. When the task is finished, have a follow-up meeting to talk about how it went, what went well, and what could be improved next time.
- You remain ultimately accountable for work you delegate so *don't* blame subordinates when things go wrong. The buck stops with you and trying to pass it sounds petty and peevish. Find out *why* mistakes were made and you can both learn from them and make sure they don't recur. It may have been your fault for not explaining clearly in the first place, or assuming that a subordinate knew something she had no way of knowing unless you told her.

- If you don't share your knowledge, you become more indispensable in your job, so people are reluctant to move you on. You have to show you're ready for more and you can't do that if you're still burdened with all the tasks you could (and should) have delegated. Don't feel insecure about this! You may be passing on knowledge but you can't pass on experience. By proving you can teach your skills to others, you're more likely to be promoted than pigeonholed.
- Delegate in plenty of time. If you've been aware for weeks of something that needs doing, no one will appreciate having the task dumped on them a couple of days before the deadline when you realize you won't get round to it after all. It's unfair and unprofessional.
- Delegating is a sign of strength, not weakness: it takes confidence in yourself and others to let bits of your job go. It doesn't mean people will think you can't cope.
- Delegate at home as well. Many women delegate effectively at work, yet go home at night and unthinkingly do all the cooking, cleaning and shopping without considering that these tasks, too, could be delegated or at least shared with partners and flatmates.

Chapter 15 / **Mastering Public Speaking**

The thought of giving presentations or speeches in front of others is something that strikes fear into the heart of many of us – in fact, surveys have pinpointed it as people's biggest fear, ahead of fear of flying or fear of spiders. But, unfortunately, public speaking is also one of the most important skills when it comes to getting on in your career, and if you want to progress, it's certain that at some stage you will be called upon to perform in public. It doesn't necessarily have to involve delivering a paper to a large conference or appearing on television, but most of us are called upon to speak up at a meeting, present a sales pitch to a new client or give a leaving speech to a colleague.

You may feel sick, panicky, wobbly, or get clammy hands and a dry throat – but so do millions of others and the ones who succeed in spite of that are those who've learned that there are ways to make things easier on yourself. You've already got the basic skill – after all, speaking is something you do every day – it just takes more confidence to extend that to speaking to a larger group. Addressing an audience is something that comes naturally to only a few, but it's something that can be learned.

As with so many things, the key to successful public speaking is adequate planning, preparation – working out what to say and how, deciding what visual aids, if any, to use, etc. – and practice.

Preparing Ahead

- What point are you aiming to get across? Who are you presenting to and what are their interests and concerns? It's important to adapt what you have to say according to your audience or you'll lose them: it's immediately obvious if you're recycling something used for someone else. There's no harm in having a basic presentation outline but the skill comes in personalizing it for each audience.

- The most boring speeches are usually those where somebody reads verbatim from a script; the most entertaining ones those where they seem to be speaking off the cuff. The first few times you do a presentation, you may find it a comfort to have your speech written out in full – but try not to use it. The best way is to know your key points off by heart (and have them written down on file cards to act as memory joggers) rather than the whole presentation. Learning everything by heart also means you're more likely to be thrown by interruptions or questions that don't fit into your scheme of things.
- Don't try to get across more than four or five key points or ideas in one speech.
- Keep notes of any hard facts or figures if you think they might elude you in the heat of the moment.
- Don't hit people with too many statistics and figures, or you'll bore the audience to tears. Use only what's relevant – the rest can be distributed on paper – which also makes them easier to understand.
- Try to grasp every opportunity to speak in public. Don't wait until you've lost your fear of it: the longer you leave it, the more your fear will grow. Start small and build up, rather than launching yourself straight into talking at a conference of 500 delegates. The first step could be something as simple as raising a point in a meeting, asking a question at a conference or introducing a speaker. Every time you do it, your confidence will grow a little.
- If you're speaking in a venue you don't know, get there early to familiarize yourself with the set-up.
- If used effectively, visual aids (slides, flip charts, videos, etc.) can bring a speech alive and give a presentation a much more professional edge. But you should be selective with them and make sure that they have earned their place, rather than just including them for the sake of it. They can be used to give light relief,

emphasize key points or clarify complicated issues. Gear your visual aids to your audience: flip charts and blackboards, for example, are no good for large numbers of people; slide projectors may be too cumbersome for a small meeting.
- If you hate the idea of all those pairs of eyes staring at you, visual aids can also be a way of diverting the audience's attention from time to time, as can asking for comments.
- Listen to other speakers and consider what it is that makes them good or bad – and learn from it.
- Rehearse out loud. Role-play in front of a friend if it helps – but don't over-rehearse or you will sound stilted. It's important to sound natural and like yourself – that way you'll come across as honest and straightforward.
- Knowing your subject inside out will give you confidence so don't agree to talk on a subject you don't understand.
- Anticipate any possible objections from your audience and aim to cover them in your presentation or at least have answers ready at the end. Acknowledging negative points proves that you've thought it through rather than just going into automatic sales-pitch mode.
- Ensure that you have enough material to fill the time: overrunning or drying up too soon will look unprofessional. As a general rule, it's better to err on the side of brevity. Rehearsing out loud is the only way to know how long your material will take to deliver. Remember to leave time for questions at the end.

Looking the Part

The initial impression you make when you walk in or stand up is vital to the success of your presentation – you'll be judged before you've even opened your mouth.
- Gear your outfit to the audience: if you're presenting to a new group of people, try to get some idea of their dress code before you go. Wearing dark, businesslike colours such as black and navy will make people take you more seriously, and you should always

go for simple, well-tailored outfits rather than anything floaty and frilly.
- Looking nervous will get you off to a bad start, so, however awful you feel, try not to let it show. Stand straight and still, with your weight equally balanced on both feet. Don't fidget around.
- Try to find out what colour background you'll be standing against: if you wear a cream jacket against a cream background, you'll disappear.
- Decide on your outfit in advance rather than frantically trying to find something on the day itself. Wear clothes in which you feel comfortable: nothing too tight (you have to be able to breathe easily) and nothing that will distract the audience from what you're saying. Don't wear something you've never worn before.
- Smile when you stand up and smile from time to time while you're talking, so you look as if you're enjoying it.

Making the Speech

- Try to get some fresh air before you talk. Do facial stretching exercises to relax tense jaw muscles.
- Remember, this isn't a matter of life or death. Don't worry that you won't be brilliant, witty and entertaining – hardly anybody is – but competence is within your grasp.
- Have a glass of water to hand in case your throat dries up with nerves. If you're using a microphone, turn away from it as you sip if you don't want amplified gulping sounds.
- Control your breathing and pause properly between sentences.
- The basic format should be: tell them what you're going to tell them; tell them; tell them what you've told them. In other words, start by summarizing what you're going to present, go into the main presentation, then recap briefly on the key points at the end.
- The first couple of minutes are vital. You have to grab people's attention straight away, so make sure your first few sentences have impact.

- Establish a relationship with your audience immediately, acknowledging that you know who they are.
- Always stand in front of your audience. If you're behind them (operating a slide projector, for instance) it's hard to keep their attention – better to use a projector with remote control.
- Don't leave a slide on when you've begun to talk about another topic: it is distracting for the audience.
- Avoid boring, long-winded anecdotes that will send everyone to sleep; keep them short and relevant and they can be useful to illustrate points or provide light relief.
- It's important to sound lively, warm and enthusiastic. Keep your intonation expressive: speaking in a monotone is guaranteed to send your audience to sleep.
- A common mistake of inexperienced speakers is to talk quickly – partly because that way the whole terrible experience will be over with sooner! Gabbling won't make a good impression, however, and people may not understand what you're saying, so make an effort to speak more slowly than normal and pause properly between sentences, or when you've finished with one point and are going to move on to another.
- If you have booked any visual aids, double check the day before that they will be there and make sure you know how to use them. Try to test them before the presentation starts: anyone can be thrown by a malfunctioning overhead projector or a flip chart that runs out of paper. Make sure that you pitch the volume of your voice to reach even the people at the back of the room; if necessary book a microphone. It's better to be too loud than too quiet.
- Make eye contact with your audience, but spread it round and include everyone. Don't just pick on one unfortunate in the nearest seat or gaze over their heads or down at your notes. Experts suggest drawing a W with your eyes across the audience. Looking up will also help your voice to project better.
- Talk as if you were speaking to a group of friends. Keep your sentences short and punchy – waffle will lose people.
- End on a positive note. Don't scuttle off the second you finish.
- Imagine how wonderful you're going to feel when you've

finished – and you will. You may still feel nervous in future but knowing that you've spoken in public before and lived to tell the tale is a huge help in giving you confidence for the next time.
- If you are particularly shy or suffer from panic attacks, take a training course to help.

GETTING AHEAD

Chapter 16 / **Learning to Assert Yourself**

Assertiveness is widely misunderstood. For many people, the word conjures up a picture of fierce, domineering women who return from assertiveness training courses and start bullying everyone. Assertiveness, however, is *not* the same as aggressiveness. It's not about being obstinate, single-minded, selfish and bossy, determined to get your own way at all costs. Rather, it's about learning to respect your own beliefs and needs and recognizing other people's rights to have beliefs and needs of their own – that may not coincide with yours. It's about making things happen rather than letting them happen to you.

It's no use just hoping that you'll get what you want. If you think you deserve a pay rise, feel a colleague isn't pulling her weight or want junior staff to improve their standards, don't just sit there and wait for them to read your mind: get assertive and *do* something about it!

Why You Should be Assertive

- The gradual build-up of frustration that results from not being assertive can lead to physical health problems such as backache, headaches, digestive problems, etc. It can also be at the root of other work problems such as poor time-management and feeling stressed. Being open and honest about your needs and opinions can prevent the build-up of that tension. If you're not assertive

enough to say no when people keep loading work on you, then something, eventually, has to give.
- Colleagues may start by sympathizing with non-assertive people but they'll soon become irritated by them, especially if they continually moan about their lot yet do nothing to change it. You can't carry on feeling sorry for people who do nothing to help themselves.
- Many women hold back from saying what they think for fear of being disliked – they hate the thought of disagreement or unpleasantness so much that they prefer to say nothing. But while ignoring conflict might make it go away in the short term, in the long term tension, anxiety and frustration increase. It's far healthier to deal with individual situations as they arise.
- Non-assertive people often delay taking decisions or tackling problems with the result that problems increase, decisions may be made too late and opportunities are lost. They are also often afraid to initiate new ways of working so that their company gets stuck with outdated methods. Most bosses *don't* want to be surrounded by yes men and women – they want people who can come up with new ideas and approaches.

How to be Assertive

- You have basic human rights: do not undervalue them. You have the right to respect from others, to hold and express your own opinions and beliefs, to ask for what you want, to refuse requests without guilt, to make mistakes.
- Be direct. How often have you been annoyed by someone pussyfooting around a subject when you wish they'd just get to the point? If you want to ask someone to do something, do it briefly and straightforwardly. Padding out requests with apologies and excuses weakens your point and confuses the listener. 'Please could you . . .' is far more effective than 'Look, I'm really sorry to bother you and I hope you don't mind – I wouldn't ask you normally, but do you think you could possibly . . .' etc.

- Self-respect is vital. Many women are brought up to believe that their needs should always come second to those of others. Don't fall into that trap: your needs are just as important as other people's and there is nothing selfish or greedy about remembering that.
- You can't expect other people to read your mind. If you don't say exactly what you'd like, how will the other person know what it is and how can they agree to it?
- If you find it difficult to ask others to do things for you, make sure beforehand that your request is justified – it's hard to be assertive when you feel guilty about asking for something to which you're not entitled.
- Learn to say no when it's appropriate. Women especially are often afraid that a refusal might cause offence and don't want to let other people down. Yes, others may be disappointed by a refusal but they will realize you're not a pushover. Soften the blow by suggesting alternatives: 'I'm afraid that I can't help tonight as I have to leave on time. However, I do have some free time tomorrow if I could be of any use then.' Don't ramble on, inventing excuses to justify your refusal. It's unnecessary and sounds unconvincing.
- Choose the right time to assert yourself. Asking the boss for a pay rise as she rushes past your desk on the way to a meeting is not a good moment to tackle it! The inevitable brush-off can set your confidence back and make it harder to broach the subject again. Instead, make an appointment with her to discuss the matter privately at a time when there won't be any distractions.
- Think positively! The frame of mind in which we approach something can often influence its outcome, so it's important to start with positive expectations.
- Visualize yourself being assertive. Think of occasions when you already practise assertiveness successfully: if you have no problems returning faulty goods to a shop, for example, then try to adopt the same mental attitude next time you need to be assertive at work.
- Learn to accept praise. If the boss says, 'I was really impressed by that progress report you did,' all you have to say is 'Thank you.

I was pleased with it too.' Don't say, 'Oh, it wasn't all that good really – I wish I was better at that sort of thing – if only I'd had a bit longer to put it together . . .'
- Aggression breeds aggression. The tougher your tactics, the tougher (you'll often find), is the resistance. Your aim should be to persuade reasonably, not to dominate.
- Think ahead: before negotiating be absolutely clear of what you want to achieve and what your rights are – and those of the other person. Rehearse your opening statements. Without thinking negatively, anticipate any possible objections and work out your responses: being prepared and having your answers ready will boost your confidence. Role-playing the situation beforehand with a friend can also help.
- Acknowledge the other person's position: 'I realize that you're overworked at the moment but this report is top priority. How do you think we should handle the situation?' This lets her know that you are not overlooking her, which will increase the chances of her responding positively. It's especially important to do this if the other person is being hostile or defensive.
- Disciplining others is something women often find hard to do, especially if the other person involved is male, but don't build up the situation in your mind to a terrifying level before it happens. If you have to criticize someone, stick to facts, not judgements. Exaggerating only weakens your argument, so avoid words like 'always', 'never' and 'impossible': they are rarely true. And there is nothing to be gained from upsetting others and putting their backs up so resist the temptation to be sarcastic or to put them down. However, try not to be apologetic or self-effacing either: if your criticism is valid, you should be able to make it confidently.
- The 'broken record' technique is useful for dealing with people who deliberately try to change the subject or convince you to do something you've said no to. Simply repeat your point, no matter what the other person says. Stay calm but firm and don't allow yourself to be sidetracked or provoked by irrelevancies. No one likes to listen to a broken record for long and the other person will eventually realize you can't be put off!

- In negotiations, aim for a win-win situation, where both parties feel they gain something. Being assertive doesn't mean forgetting about compromise, and a truly assertive person will look for common ground, not try to bulldoze her own way through. Don't forget to recognize other people's rights as well as asserting your own.
- Control your body language. Avoid actions which give a non-assertive message such as downcast eyes, twiddling fingers, jiggling legs. Look up at people and maintain firm eye contact, but not a fixed glare. Posture should be upright but relaxed; shoulders down, not hunched; arms by your side, not crossed defensively.
- Your tone of voice is as important as what you say. Keep your voice firm but not hostile, your speech fluent and free of hesitation. Speak up – don't whine or whisper. People often reveal nervousness by talking rapidly so make a conscious effort to slow down a little. Avoid using non-assertive words such as 'only', 'rather' and 'maybe'.
- When asking for a pay rise, remember that you're not begging for a favour but asking for a reasonable reward for all you do for your employer. Be confident about your own worth and make a list of any new skills or responsibilities you've acquired, as well as any specific contributions you've made to the company's success. Find out the going rate for the job: could you leave and get much higher pay somewhere else? It may be unwise to threaten to leave (unless you don't mind if they call your bluff) but it's often the case that companies appreciate their staff only when they've been offered a new job elsewhere.
- In meetings, don't be afraid to raise apparently obvious points because you assume other people must have already thought of them. We all think differently and what is obvious to you isn't necessarily obvious to others. Keep your contributions brief and to the point – don't stray off into irrelevant issues. Don't allow people to interrupt you and equally don't interrupt others.
- Accept that being assertive won't automatically get you everything you want and don't be afraid of failure. Don't ask for too much at once: setting realistic goals reduces the chances of failure and consequent lack of confidence.

- Don't take all refusals and disagreements personally. It isn't necessarily an attack on you if someone feels differently about your work suggestions. Remember to judge other people's proposals objectively too, and don't attack them on the basis of personal dislike.
- Try to see the other person's point of view and understand their position. Keep calm, stay as objective as possible and explain the situation from your perspective.
- You may find that the new, assertive you makes other people a bit nervous at first. That's the price you pay for increased self-confidence and respect.
- Assertiveness is external *and* internal. It's not enough just to sound the part: you have to feel it to carry it through. Don't rely on praise from others to build up your confidence: learn to applaud yourself when you know you've done something well.
- The first time you assert yourself *will* be terrifying but, as in everything else, you'll improve with practice. You'll find that behaving assertively leads to increased self-confidence and that in turn will lead to more assertive behaviour.

Chapter 17 / **What Makes You Promotable?**

If you want to get ahead, the key thing to realize is that it's up to *you*. No one else cares as much about your career as you do, so don't just expect other people to notice you and offer you things. If you want something, take action to get it. If you're passive and wait for things to happen to you, you run the risk that they might pass you by instead. You have to take responsibility for your future, get yourself noticed and make the opportunities.

How to be Visible

The first thing to realize is that just being good at your job isn't enough. More importantly, you have to be *seen* to be good at it, so do what you can to bring yourself to the attention of people in positions of power.

• Volunteer to sit on company committees, undertake projects or train junior members of the department. Enthusiasm is always valued by employers.
• Learn to speak well in public. Giving presentations and talks, both in-house and to outside bodies, is one of the quickest and best ways to raise your profile.
• Always put your name to any report you write, so that it's obvious who deserves the credit.
• Let management know you're interested in training opportunities and keen to develop your skills. Tell them you want to get ahead. If your company has a formal appraisal system, you'll get your chance to make your views heard in your interview; if not, set up an appointment with your boss to talk about your career progress.

Networking

Good contacts are one of the keys to career success, so networking with colleagues and others in the business is crucial. This can mean joining an industry body or women's support group, or simply making a point of maintaining contacts with former colleagues.
* Always try to attend company functions, training seminars and industry events and make sure that your face becomes known to the right people.
* Always carry business cards with you. Every single person you meet is a potential source of help, information and contacts. They can also be a support to you, which is especially important when you're working in a field largely dominated by men where at times you might feel a little isolated.
* Networking isn't just about meeting people in other companies, it's also important to network within your own organization and get to know people in different departments. You could, for example, suggest that all the PAs in the company get together over lunch once a month, so you can compare ways of working, give each other helpful tips and find out more about how other departments work.
* Don't think networking is confined to high-powered executives. It's an important resource for staff at any level.
* Remember that to get the most out of networking, you have to be prepared to put as much in as you take out. You can't ask others for help and advice all the time unless you're prepared to do the same for them.

How to Impress the Boss

Apart from mastering such key skills as public speaking and business writing (covered in chapters 6 to 15), the main thing that sets you apart is attitude.

- Make a point of finding out your boss's personal work hates, and what she admires in staff. It's fairly safe to say that all bosses appreciate someone who is decisive, conscientious, thorough, shows initiative and doesn't make a mountain out of a molehill. And they all hate anyone being lazy, wasting time, shirking responsibility or being slapdash.
- Give added value – always put in more than you're asked to.
- Enjoy your work and be seen to enjoy it.
- Be loyal to the boss, the team and the organization.
- Make your job as important as you can and try to take on more responsibility – that way you become more valuable to the company and show that you're capable of more.
- Be positive at work. If there's anything you're not happy about, suggest ways to change instead of moaning. Always look for solutions rather than problems.
- Keep a promise, however small. Make a point of returning anything you borrow from colleagues, even if it's only a pencil: being reliable on small matters gives other people greater confidence in your ability to come up with the goods on the big things.
- Avoid clutter where possible and keep your desk tidy. Don't leave it a tip at the end of the day. Process paperwork quickly and efficiently.
- Understand that it's a business first, and that money is the bottom line. Always think whether there is a faster, cheaper, more efficient way of doing things. Every company likes employees who can save them time and money.
- Be prepared to take calculated risks; be innovative and confident in your approach to new projects.
- Be flexible – with people, with your approach to problems and with the work you are prepared to take on.
- Become an expert in something.
- Be a self-starter and show initiative.
- Get your time under control. (See chapter 11 for time-management tips.)
- Never lose your temper.

- Always meet a deadline – and if you can't, tell people as early as possible. Missing a deadline without warning will create a bad impression and the knock-on effect can be disastrous.
- Always be early, even if it's only five or ten minutes.
- Try not to bring your personal life to work.
- Never make snap judgements about other people.
- Cultivate a positive self-image. If you run yourself down or refuse to accept praise, that will be reflected in the way other people perceive you. But when you have strong self-esteem and feel good about yourself, it encourages others to look at you in a favourable light too.

Winning at Office Politics

It's also important to be aware of office politics because, like it or not, they're a fact of working life and can affect the progress you make. The sooner you learn to play the game and understand the rules, the better.

- Never betray a confidence or spread malicious gossip: if you do you'll lose the trust of friends and colleagues for ever.
- Don't turn your nose up at all gossip, though. It's important to know what's going on at work and sometimes the informal office grapevine is the only way to find out.
- Remember that personal gossip has a horrible way of finding its way back to the person you're talking about. Don't say anything you wouldn't stand by or anything that could hurt another person.
- Don't give away confidential business decisions to *anyone*: you might think it's OK to tell a friend, but they might have a friend who has a friend who works for one of your rivals, to whom the information could be highly useful and you could damage your company as a result.
- The more senior you are, the more important it is to realize the importance of confidentiality.
- If you hear a rumour that, if true, could affect your job, don't

just stew about it. Talk to your department head immediately and ask her whether or not it's true.
- Never reveal a source: you could get someone else into trouble.
- Be discerning and be careful whom you trust. If you're not sure of someone's discretion, don't tell them anything that could harm you.
- If you hear a rumour that you know is untrue, quash it.
- Accept that you won't necessarily be loved by all, especially as you climb the ladder, but if you are consistently pleasant to and professional with all your colleagues, you should avoid positive enmity.
- Don't save your good behaviour for your superiors alone: treat everybody courteously and with respect, whatever their level of seniority.
- Make sure you get ahead on your own merits, not by sticking the knife in anyone else's back. Treat others as you would like to be treated yourself.
- If there are difficulties with colleagues, tackle them rather than letting them fester. See chapter 19 for advice on dealing with difficult people.
- Never take credit that rightly belongs to someone else.

Plan for Promotion

- Think ahead. If you want to be posted abroad in a few years' time, start learning the language *now*: don't leave it till you apply for the job. If you are seen to have certain skills, it's more likely that eventually you'll be chosen for that job.
- If you want to become a manager, start acting like one.
- Look at the person who's doing the job you want. Try to work out what it is that they do and why they're good at it.
- Make sure you look the part – dress as if you were doing the job that's the next one up from you. (See chapter 23 on the importance of image.)

- Don't just keep your eyes down, concentrating on the task in hand. Keep looking outwards at what's happening around you.
- Think long-term. Everyone has to start at the bottom so don't worry if your first job seems too lowly – it's a start. The important thing is to keep your eye on where you want to be and make sure that it's taking you in the right direction.
- Be persistent. Every career has its upsets and setbacks, and things don't always come as quickly as you think they should or as soon as you deserve. Patience, determination and resilience are key qualities to cultivate.
- Keep up to date with industry issues, reading professional magazines and papers, so that you understand how you and your company fit into the greater scheme of things and what's going to be happening in the future.
- Take regular checks of your career progress to make sure you're staying on track. (See chapter 20 for tips on doing a career appraisal.)

How *Not* to Impress the Boss

As well as making a note of all the things you should do to get ahead at work, perhaps it's helpful to look, too, at the things you should definitely *not* do. Here, then, are some surefire ways to put yourself in the doghouse . . .

- Frequently arrive late at work and offer no explanation for doing so.
- Often fail to turn up at all.
- Fall into a regular habit of taking Fridays and Mondays off 'sick'.
- Blame a mistake on a colleague.
- Get involved in a feud with a colleague and create office tension.
- Spread malicious gossip.
- Wine and dine friends on expenses.
- Casually mention your company is in financial difficulties to a rival at a business drinks party.

- Get drunk at work.
- Get drunk at a work social event and tell everyone there you hate your job.
- Steal office stationery.
- Steal *anything*.
- Spend hours on the phone making personal calls and screaming, 'He *didn't!*' at regular intervals.
- Sigh and say you're busy when your boss asks for help.
- Roll your eyes if asked to do anything outside your job description.
- Show no effort whatsoever to try to improve your work.
- Hide a particularly difficult project at the back of your drawer and pretend that it simply doesn't exist.
- Phone in sick when you've just bought a flat needing renovation.
- Make it clear you would rather be doing almost anything else.
- Bring your personal life to work.
- Regard your colleagues as adversaries rather than team players.
- Criticize your boss's work without being constructive.
- Ignore orders from your boss and work only on what you want to.
- Tell your boss that this job is a mere stopgap before getting the position you *really* want.
- Photocopy thirty CVs and then leave them lying on your desk.
- Take three-hour lunch breaks.
- Spend your spare moments reading a paperback or filing your nails.
- Have an affair with a senior colleague who is responsible for the hiring and firing.
- Think you are better than your boss – and tell everyone.
- Constantly fail to deliver when others are relying on you.
- Always be in the wrong place at the wrong time.
- Show little interest in any department not related to your own.
- Allow a worrying situation to escalate and then refuse to ask for help.
- Shrug off the responsibility when a project goes wrong.

- Take on freelance work when your contract specifically forbids it.
- Find out how much your colleagues earn and constantly make reference to it.
- Give less than 100 per cent.
- Make sexist/racist remarks.
- Claim you are computer literate in an interview, then arrive on the first day and ask someone how to turn on the screen.
- Spend hours gossiping by the coffee machine.
- Forget the slides when you and five colleagues arrive in Hamburg for a presentation to a prospective client.
- Spend company money on new equipment without authorization.
- Think spelling mistakes and dog-eared documents don't matter much.
- Dress inappropriately, despite your company's strict dress code.
- Crunch crisps and answer the phone with a 'Yeah?' when the MD rings to speak to your boss.
- Undermine your boss in front of other people.
- Leave confidential documents lying around the photocopier.
- Keep a personal crisis to yourself and assume you can cope without your work suffering.
- Be the last to arrive and the first to leave every day.
- Laugh when your boss talks about cost-cutting measures.
- Act resentful and uninterested when people try to teach you something new.
- Always be late.
- Lose your temper.

Chapter 18 / **Getting a Pay Rise**

In the heydays of the eighties, an annual increase was taken by many employees as an automatic right. Now, after years of recession and cost-cutting, it's no longer something we can take for granted so, like it or not, if you want a rise you'll probably have to ask for it. In some areas, such as education and medicine, salary ranges may be fixed but in most other cases money is negotiable.

Asking your boss for money is a fairly daunting prospect – but so is continuing to feel under-valued and under-appreciated in your work. If you feel you're not being paid enough for the job you do, then you're entitled to say so – and don't assume that your boss will laugh in your face. The important thing is to follow a few basic rules and tackle her in the right way . . .

- Timing is important. If you've just been praised for a job well done, or recently undertaken a major project, it's a good time to ask, while your personal profile is high. On the other hand, if you know the company is doing badly, maybe you should wait until things start to pick up. Some experts suggest finding out when your company's financial year-end is and asking right at the start of the next year, before all the money's been allocated elsewhere.
- Arrange a proper meeting with your boss to discuss your pay. Don't tackle her by the coffee machine or as she's passing your desk.
- Do some research to find out what other people in similar jobs are paid, both within the company and in other organizations. Contact industry bodies or trade organizations to see if they have any figures on salary levels or recommended rates of pay. Unless it's absolutely unavoidable, try not to compare your salary with someone else's within the company: however ridiculous you think

it is, most employers don't look kindly upon employees discussing their salaries.
- Before you ask for a rise, draw up a list of reasons why you deserve it. Compile a list of your achievements and successes over the past year, particularly any ways in which you've saved the company money, increased profits or won clients. If they look really impressive, type them up and hand the list to your boss. What do you bring to the job? What especially valuable skills do you have? When was your last pay rise and how much was it? How have your duties and responsibilities increased since then? What have you achieved for the company in the past year? What extra duties would you be prepared to take on?
- Prepare your arguments and how you want to put them across and rehearse them before your meeting.
- Don't justify your request for a rise by saying you need to buy a car, you're overdrawn or your mortgage has gone up. You have to convince your employer that you *deserve* extra money, not just that you want or need it.
- Have confidence: if you want to convince others you're worth more money, you have to believe it yourself. It's important to think positive: the more confident, assertive and enthusiastic you sound, the better your chances of getting your rise.
- If your boss says that she can't make any exception to the 3 per cent rise that everyone else in the company is getting, you have to have arguments prepared as to why you *should* be an exception.
- Don't feel embarrassed or guilty about talking about money – at the end of the day, that's what everyone's in business for, your boss just as much as everyone else.
- Keep negotiations friendly and avoid complaining or whining: treat this as a chance to show how committed you are to the job and the organization.
- Ask for more than you want and be prepared to settle for less. Would you consider increased perks, such as a car, luncheon vouchers, reduced hours, extra training, etc., instead of a cash increase?

- If your boss won't give you a rise now, ask when she thinks the situation might change, or what she feels you would have to do to merit one.
- If you have been offered a new job and a higher salary elsewhere, don't be afraid to mention it but don't make it a threat. Explain that you are highly attached to your present company and don't really want to move, but that the other offer is financially tempting. It will cost an employer more to go through the costly process of recruiting and training a new member of staff than it will to give you a rise.
- Don't deliver an ultimatum unless you're prepared to carry it through. It's fine to say you'll have to go if you don't get a rise – but then you'll have to stick to it.
- If you are successful, great – but keep it to yourself. Don't go out and brag to everybody else: they may feel jealous and your boss won't be impressed.
- Once you've agreed on a rise, ask for written confirmation as soon as possible.
- If your boss refuses to give you more money, even though you know the company is prospering, you're working hard and you've presented your case well, maybe it's time to leave.
- You're more likely to get a big salary rise by moving from one company to another than by staying where you are. The longer you stay with one employer the more likely it is that your salary will be falling below the going rate for the job.
- Your employers are breaking the law if they pay a man doing the same job more than they are paying you. If this is the case, contact the Equal Opportunities Commission for advice (0161-833 9244). You may also have grounds for a claim if you're doing work of equal value.
- If applicable, contact your union for help and advice. If your employer recognizes a union, being a member may entitle you to automatic minimum salary brackets.

Chapter 19 / **Dealing with Difficult People**

'Hell is other people,' said Jean-Paul Sartre – and there are times during the working day when most of us would agree with him. It doesn't matter how wonderful your job in theory, in reality the people you work with can turn it into a nightmare: aggressive bosses whose unpredictable temper tantrums leave you trembling, manipulative colleagues who try to offload their work on to you, irate customers who vent their anger and frustration on you as your company's representative. The stress of coping with such difficult people can adversely affect your work and should not be under-estimated.

It may not always be possible to control other people's behaviour but we *can* control our own reactions to that behaviour and the attitude we adopt can have a knock-on effect on others. Next time somebody at work is bothering you, step back, take a cool look at the situation and follow these tips for tackling it.

- It's hard to look at ourselves objectively, but before you blame everyone else for being difficult, make sure it isn't your own attitude that's at fault. At the same time, don't be so self-effacing that you assume you must be the cause of the problems. Is there something about your manner or behaviour that could be affecting this person's view of you? If there's room for doubt, consider how you could make yourself easier to work with.
- Understanding what you're dealing with is the first step towards sorting it out so try to work out *why* the other person is behaving in this way. Look for reasons (such as fear, anxiety, guilt) that may be causing the problem behaviour.
- Watch your communication skills – too many problems are the result of a simple misunderstanding that gets out of hand. Words mean different things to different people and the communication

gap can be particularly wide between men and women, or between people from different cultural backgrounds and upbringings. Just being aware of the fact that we have different ways of speaking will help. (See chapter 6 for tips on improving your communication skills.)

- Act naturally with superiors. Rather than kowtowing to them or retreating shyly into your shell, try to see them as equals and treat them as you would like to be treated.
- Don't procrastinate. If someone upsets you, do something about it straight away. Don't put it off, telling yourself that you'll say something if it happens again. Deal with it now and you may prevent it happening again or getting worse. It's easier to deal with problems as they arise rather than waiting for frustration to build up to fever pitch.
- Avoid public confrontation. Set a time to speak privately to the person, rather than embarrassing her – and maybe yourself – in front of an audience. Choose a quiet time when you can both give the talk your full attention. If you're worried, role-play with a friend beforehand.
- Be positive and concentrate on behaviour that the person can do something about. Focus on the point in hand and don't get sidetracked into other issues. Don't make personal attacks.
- Avoid sounding accusatory: simply state what the problem is and why it concerns you. Stick to facts, not emotions. Explain how you think matters might be improved but be open to alternative solutions. *Listen* to what the other person has to say.
- If you really can't handle a face-to-face approach, write a letter or memo to the person, explaining how you feel.
- If you find it difficult to tackle other people in this way, then it's time you learned to be more assertive. There are plenty of books and courses (your local library will have details) available to teach you the basic techniques (and you'll find advice in chapter 16).
- Don't moan to other people about how much someone annoys you if you haven't first given that person a chance to put matters right. Unless you tell her about it, she may not even be aware that she's annoying you.

- Don't assume that behaviour which you find 'obviously irritating' is deliberate. We all see things differently and something that annoys you might not bother another person. Ask colleagues if they find this person a problem, too: their support can be a great help and they may have good advice on how to cope. Letting off steam with other people may be all you need to do to alleviate the situation – but be careful not to turn into a lynch mob.
- Keep a cool head. Confrontation may help you in the short term but it usually leaves you feeling guilty and ashamed. It also leaves the other person wary of you and has a negative effect on future dealings with her. It isn't always easy to keep your emotions in check, especially if you feel you're being unfairly dealt with, but emotional reactions at work are generally counter-productive. Tears and tantrums are not professional and will lose you the respect of others.
- We often react in ways that make a situation worse: getting defensive instead of looking at an issue clearly; taking matters personally when that wasn't intended; getting angry or sarcastic when we're hurt. These are natural reactions but they don't help anyone.
- Recognize that sometimes, whatever you do, the problem won't go away. If people continue to be difficult, you may have to go to somebody else in your organization who has the power to influence them – your head of department or personnel officer.
- If the problem continues, keep a log of the difficult behaviour, noting down any incidents which distress you. Include dates, times and witnesses' names, if any. Detail what happened and how it made you feel. You'll need this as evidence if it comes to a disciplinary hearing.
- If you are a member of a union, ask them for advice. In the case of sexual or racial harassment, contact the Equal Opportunities Commission (0161-833 9244). You may also be able to get advice from your local Citizens' Advice Bureau (listed in *Yellow Pages*).

Manipulative People

- Some people use emotional blackmail to get their way, trying to force you to do something by making you feel guilty if you don't. Don't give in to them. If their request is unreasonable, your refusal is justified and there's no reason to feel guilty about it.
- Saying no to such people may be difficult at first but persevere: it will make them realize they can't walk all over you and lessen the chances of them trying it on again.
- A manipulative boss may play on your loyalty, refusing you the promotion you deserve by convincing you you're far too valuable where you are. Recognize this for the selfish behaviour it really is and don't let it hold you back.

Handling Anger

- If a person attacks you verbally, don't automatically leap to the defensive – it's a natural reaction, and hard to resist at first, but practise restraint.
- Don't take anger personally. You may be the person bearing the brunt of it but remember that it is usually the result of frustration about the situation and not aimed specifically at you.
- Take a constructive approach and concentrate on solving the other person's problem. If someone is angry with you, you have the right to know why. Don't be afraid to ask the other person to explain further. Listen carefully to find out what is wrong and ask questions to clarify the situation. Maintain eye contact.
- Summarize the situation as you see it without being sarcastic or condescending. This shows you have been listening and makes sure that you understand the situation. Too often problems arise because we make assumptions about what we *think* the other person means.
- Don't get defensive or pass the buck. An irate client doesn't care

whose fault it is that things have gone wrong; she just wants to know what you're going to do to put things right. She will react more positively to someone who's obviously trying to help her.
- Recognize that anger may be the expression of fear, anxiety, guilt or frustration. Cliché as it sounds, aggressive people may be hiding their lack of basic self-confidence behind a tough exterior.
- Watch your timing. If, for example, you know your boss is always bad-tempered first thing in the morning, try to reduce contact with her until after lunch. Or if you know that her day gets increasingly hectic as it gets later, don't bother her with petty problems at five o'clock.
- Listen before you act. Stand back from the other person's anger and allow her to get things off her chest fully before you start trying to work things out. Don't tell her to calm down or lower her voice before she's had a chance to express herself.
- It's hard not to feel hurt about unjustified anger, but don't take it personally and don't react emotionally. People may vent their anger on you because they're afraid to show it to the person who's actually causing it. Your boss, for example, may be unpleasant to you because *her* boss has just annoyed her but she felt unable to confront her about it; it's easier for her to transfer her feelings to you.
- Don't retaliate by getting angry yourself: you'll probably end up in a mutual slanging match, going nowhere but down. Yes, you should express your own feelings, but in a cool, rational way. Be aware of the pitch and volume of your voice.
- Don't apologize when you don't really understand why she's angry. Don't sulk and don't get uptight.
- Sarcasm is an indirect form of aggression. Designed to make others feel inferior, it is often used by people who may feel uncertain themselves. Getting defensive or showing that you're hurt is playing into their hands. The best way to cope is to take the fun out of it for them; ignore it or tackle it head on by asking them *why* they said what they did or felt the need to be sarcastic. Bite back the temptation to be sarcastic yourself.
- If you have an aggressive boss, find out if her behaviour is

affecting other employees too. If so, and if speaking to her directly doesn't work, you may have to go to her superior or to the personnel department. Stick to facts when explaining what's wrong; have details of specific incidents and their cost to the company.

Passive People

- Bad at expressing their own needs and wants, passive people (often women) tend to submit to those of others while resentment simmers beneath the surface. It's no use forcing a confrontation with people like this; they'll simply retreat further into their shells and become more martyrish than ever.
- Some people may be just as angry as the person who rants and raves but won't show it directly. Learn to read the signs as to what lies beneath the words: people's body language often contradicts what they say and passive people especially may give away what they really feel in their non-verbal signals. Look for sure-fire signs of tension, such as tapping fingers or feet, clenched jaw, rapid speech, raised voice, fiddling with jewellery or avoiding eye contact.
- Afraid of hurting anyone's feelings or worried that you won't like them if they disagree, passive people won't be direct about what they want. Instead, they drop hints or expect you to read their mind, then sulk when you don't get it right. They need to be encouraged to be more open. Explain that you want to do your best for them but that you find it hard to know without being told what they want: it would be easier for you and better for them if they could tell you openly.
- Give credit where it's due. Passive people, especially, need reassurance. A few words of appreciation take up little of your time but can mean a lot to them and will encourage them to do even more. Lack of recognition may make them feel like not bothering next time you want something doing.
- Passive people often suffer from feelings of insecurity, inferiority and lack of self-confidence. Encourage them by helping them to understand that they'll attract respect by being more assertive.

Chapter 20 / **Keeping on Track of Your Career Goals**

Successful careers don't just happen, they need to be nurtured so it's important to keep evaluating and re-evaluating your career as you progress. You need to have a plan and to keep referring back to it to check how reality is matching up. Too many people tend to be reactive rather than proactive, hoping that solutions will emerge and waiting for something to turn up without actually trying to make it happen. Setting goals helps you feel stronger, more confident and more in control and gives you a sense of direction rather than meandering along at work.

Think back over the past twelve months and consider what you've achieved in that time. If your overriding feeling is, 'Oh, God! Another year gone and I still haven't been promoted/got that salary increase/found a new job,' then set aside some time to take stock and do a career appraisal (birthdays and New Years are good natural turning points to get yourself motivated). It will cost you nothing but time and should pay real dividends before the next year comes around.

Getting Started

- Before you plan ahead, look at where you are now. What are your basic responsibilities at work? How well do you fulfil them? Would you be missed if you left? Look back over the past year. What progress have you made? What could you have done better? Have you acquired any new skills? What did you find disappointing? Concentrate on the positive and remember to include your

whole life, not just work. When thinking of the disappointments, look at what you've learned from them rather than dwelling on the negative.
- Now consider how well the job suits you. How satisfied are you with your salary, title, hours and holiday allowance? Are you happy with the physical surroundings in which you work? Do you feel comfortable with the company dress code? What do you least and most enjoy about your work? Be specific. Clarify your feelings by asking yourself the following questions:

   What are you doing now that you want to do more of in future?
   What are you doing now that you *don't* want to do any more?
   What are you *not* doing now that you would like to do?
   What have you done in the past that you know you *never* want to do again?
   What *should* you be doing that you really want to do?
   What should you be doing that you *don't* want to do?

- Once you're clear how you feel about the job, you need to be equally clear about your personal assets. Do you have a good memory? The ability to write clearly? Are you competent with numbers or good at passing knowledge to others? Draw up a list of key business skills (e.g., initiative, reliability, time-management, decision-making, interpersonal skills) and assess your performance in each area, rating yourself as good, average or poor. The aim is to recognize your good points and pinpoint your weaker areas so that you can work on strengthening them. If you want an objective view (and can take it), ask a friend or colleague for her opinion.
- If you're confident that you're working in the right field, then look around your organization to see how you could fit in there and where the next step up is. Is the company planning to expand into any new areas that could throw up some fresh job opportunities?
- Look at the person directly above you at work. Do you want her job and, if so, are you likely to be offered it if she leaves? If the answer to either of these questions is no, then you have to ask yourself why you're staying in your current position and what it is you're working towards. If you're happy where you are, fine. If

not, it may be time to move on, either to a new company or in a completely new direction (see chapter 26).
- Be realistic about your industry's future – does it have one or is it a dying field? Are you narrowing your future options too much the longer you stay in your current role? Remember that staying too long in the same job can be perceived by potential employers as just as much of a bad thing as changing too often. And the danger of letting yourself get stuck too long is that you start to lose confidence in your ability to do anything else.
- If there have already been redundancies at work, are you sure that your job is really safe? It's always wise to keep an eye on trends and to think about how they might affect you, so that you can futureproof yourself. You have to be adaptable: you may not like the prospect of change, but if you don't want to get left behind, you have to be prepared for it.
- If you really can't decide what you want to do, start building your skills portfolio anyway, by learning a language or taking a computing course, for example. Every extra skill you acquire will stand you in good stead while you're making up your mind.

Setting Goals

Once you've decided the direction you want your career to go in, the next step is to draw up a viable plan to get you there. After all, appraisals are only effective if you use them as building blocks for the future. If you want to succeed, it's vital to set goals. They provide a structure for monitoring your progress, focusing your attention and keeping you active in making sure your career's still on track. With a clear goal in mind you're far more likely to make progress.
- Set yourself a major objective. Decide, for example, where you want to be in five years' time. Then break that down into a series of smaller, less intimidating chunks, with a target date for completing each one. You need to have short-term, medium-term and long-term goals – say, completing a business report by the end of

the week so you can relax over the weekend (short), becoming one of your company's top ten sales people by the end of the year (medium) or setting up your own business within the next five years (long).
• Don't procrastinate: put your plan into action straight away. The first step can be as simple as writing a letter or making an appointment. Each short-term goal reached brings the bigger goal more clearly into focus and gives you a sense of achievement that encourages you to tackle the next step.
• Achieving a goal is a reward in itself, but if you feel it will help, give yourself other incentives too: 'If I get that promotion by the end of the year, I'll treat myself to a really good quality suit,' etc. Allow yourself a pat on the back when you accomplish something, and rejoice in the congratulations of others.
• Self-discipline and motivation are important. If you have a concrete object in mind (say, a Caribbean holiday or a new house) that you want to have by the end of the year, stick a picture of it up somewhere like the fridge door so that you're constantly reminded of what you're working towards.
• There's no harm in aiming high – research shows that people with high expectations generally do better than those with low ones – but don't set your sights *too* high. Goal-setting must be realistic. It's a good idea to set yourself targets that will stretch you a little, but if they are way over the top they will only demotivate you when you don't achieve them. On the other hand, don't let realistic mean thinking small and setting targets so low that you settle for less than you should get.
• Don't let yourself be influenced by peer pressure or what you feel you *ought* to want. You may, for example, feel obliged to chase promotion or more money, when what you really want is to reduce your working hours and have more time for outside interests. Don't feel you have to be high-powered if that's not what would make you happy. It could be that you are progressing towards job satisfaction and/or a better quality of life.
• Be honest with yourself – there's no point in setting goals that you know you don't want badly enough to do what it takes

to achieve them. Set lots of goals then choose the half-dozen or so that you want most and concentrate on those. If you give yourself too many, you'll lose focus and probably not reach any of them.
- Make your dreams active: instead of dreaming about *being* a millionaire, dream about *doing* something that will make you one.
- Make sure your goals are SMART – Specific, Measurable, Achievable, Realistic and Time-scaled.

Staying on Track

- Keep a written log of your goals, so that you have a record of what you're aiming for, and how far you achieved them. Mental goals can be forgotten, but if they're there in black and white, it can be sobering at the end of the year to look at the list and find you've achieved nothing on it.
- Don't just sit back and feel pleased that you've completed a thorough career appraisal then forget all about it until the end of next year. One of the most important things about goal-setting is remembering to review the objectives you set. Anyone can come up with a list of goals, but you should set aside some time, say once a month, to check your list and see how far you're getting. If it helps, have a goal-setting session with a friend and meet up once a month to check progress.
- Keep evaluating your progress as the year goes on. The workplace is constantly changing and the objectives you set at the start of the year may suddenly cease to be relevant. You have to be able to adapt your goals as necessary. In the same way, your needs and priorities may change and there is nothing wrong with deciding that a certain objective isn't for you, after all. Making the decision to abandon a particular goal isn't the same as failing. The key lies in being able to recognize where you are going to be happiest.

Clearing Hurdles

- You also need to accept that while there are some obstacles you can overcome, such as lack of training or experience, others may be much more difficult. For example, if there is someone in the job above you who's obviously there for life, don't waste time waiting for the move that will never come.
- It's important not to dwell on disappointments. Remind yourself that nobody gets everything right all the time, even if it sometimes seems as if they do. Learn from your mistakes: find out why you went wrong and let that be a spur to do better next time rather than an excuse for giving up. But the most important thing is to make a start. Worrying about how difficult things may be is far worse than actually doing them.

Further Information

If your main problem in setting goals is deciding what you want to do, you might benefit from a visit to a careers office or careers consultant, who can provide a mixture of testing and counselling to try to find the direction you should head in. You'll find companies listed under Careers Advice in *Yellow Pages*. The type of service provided, and the cost, varies greatly, so ask for an estimate first and a full description of what you get for your money.

Chapter 21 / **Handling Stress**

A little stress can be good for you, stimulating you to meet challenges and achieve ambitions. However, when it goes into overdrive, your health, mental attitude and work performance may begin to suffer, so it's important to keep stress levels under control, and learn how to cope when it all gets too much.

- Poor time-management is a key cause of stress: if you have too much work and not enough time to do it, you're bound to end up feeling the strain. See chapter 11 for tips on how to get your time under control, and chapter 12 for help in learning to prioritize.
- Is there anything you could delegate to somebody else? See chapter 14 for advice on delegating effectively.
- Recognize that we all have different stress thresholds. Some of us can handle less pressure than others, so it's important to ensure that you're in the right kind of job for you – no point in looking for work in the City if you'll end up overwrought.
- Know your own limits and learn to say no when you genuinely can't take any more on.
- Look out for the warning signs of stress (see box) and deal with them straight away. Don't allow the situation to escalate.
- Find a system of relaxation that works for you to help you unwind after work, whether it's playing a game of squash, practising yoga or having a massage.
- Avoid leaning on artificial stimulants such as tea and coffee, cigarettes, alcohol or tranquillizers. They may give you temporary respite but won't deal with the root of the problem. Whatever is causing the stress will still be there.
- Find ways to relax during the day. Take an exercise class at lunchtime, go swimming before work, get out and go for a walk around the block.

Warning signs of stress

sleeplessness • lethargy • lack of enthusiasm • irritability • mood swings • stomach upsets • panic attacks • muscle tension • weight loss or gain • breathlessness • weakness • losing your temper or bursting into tears for no real reason • inability to concentrate or to make decisions • aching limbs • fatigue • drinking or smoking more

- Look after your physical health. Get plenty of sleep. Eat at regular times and make sure you have a well-balanced diet. Pay particular attention to the amounts of B and C vitamins, calcium, zinc and iron you're getting.
- If you are feeling stressed, you may make matters worse by hyperventilating (breathing too quickly and shallowly). This can cause all kinds of symptoms, from constriction in the chest to migraine, upset stomach and panic feelings. Practise simple breathing exercises to calm you down, and make a point of doing them when you are about to make a difficult phone call, speak up in a large meeeting or give a presentation. Place one hand on your upper chest and the other just above your navel. Then inhale slowly and deeply enough to feel most of the movement in your abdomen rather than in your chest. Aim to take only eight to ten breaths a minute.
- If you're worried because you're being asked to undertake a task you've never done before or to use machinery with which you're not familiar, speak up. It is always better to admit you don't know how to do something than to blunder ahead and make a mess of things. Ask someone to explain the procedure to you and take notes. Find out if there are any relevant training courses the company could send you on, so that you are better equipped to do the job.
- If you're worried about what others are thinking of your performance, ask for feedback. If it's positive, stop worrying. If there

are negative points, work on putting them right – and stop worrying!

- Unlikely as it sounds, not having enough to do or being bored in your work can be stressful. It can make you feel unproductive and unimportant. Let your department head know that you do not have enough work to keep you occupied or to challenge you and ask if there is anything else you could be helping out with. If not, it's probably time to look for a new job.
- Living under fear of redundancy or being sacked is stressful – but worrying is a complete waste of energy. If the signs are that there will be redundancies at work, channel your energy into preparing for the changes and investigating other avenues for the future. Are there openings in other departments? Get your CV ready.
- Perfectionists are often stressed because they feel everything they do could have been done better and they worry about failing. As a result, they tend to leave things to the last minute, so that when they run out of time and simply have to do the task quickly and under pressure, they have the excuse that it's not perfect because they didn't have enough time to do it! But they're just perpetuating the problem. It's better to stop setting impossibly high standards for yourself and realize that the world won't fall apart if something is slightly less than perfect. You increase stress by putting something off, and having it hanging over your head for longer, rather than getting it out of the way.
- Talk to other people: sharing things can help to relieve stress. However, if something is really bothering you at work, don't carry on complaining about it to colleagues and friends – talk to your manager or someone with the authority to do something about it.
- If something in your personal life, such as separation from a partner or the illness of a parent, is causing stress, tell your boss: if you don't and if your performance is below par as a result of the problem, they may assume you're not up to the job.
- Always take your full holiday allowance. Whatever you think, you're not indispensable and you *need* to take time away from work to keep your life in balance.

- Don't take on all the responsibility at home on top of your job. If you're living with someone else, then work such as shopping, cleaning, etc., should be shared equally. You're doing yourself no favours if you let others get away without pulling their weight.

Chapter 22 / **Workplace Health**

Your building may be a dream to look at – but is it a nightmare to work in? If your physical environment at work is unhealthy it's difficult to perform well. Too much noise, poor ventilation, bad lighting, low humidity, high temperatures, low temperatures – they can all take their toll and get on top of you. You may feel lethargic and tired all the time, get constant headaches or seem to have a permanent cold.

If you think your office is making you ill, perhaps it's time to remind your boss that Sick Building Syndrome, which has been recognized by the World Health Organization since 1982, results in reduced staff efficiency, increased absenteeism and staff turnover, and time lost in dealing with complaints.

Air Quality

- If it hasn't already been done, take steps to make your office a non-smoking zone. If smokers object, perhaps a room somewhere in the building could be set aside for smoking. Make sure that any smoking areas are detached from the main ventilation system to prevent recycling smoke.
- Get some greenery in. As well as making the office look more attractive, plants help to purify and humidify the air.
- VDUs, photocopiers and other office equipment make the air dryer and churn out positive ions instead of the invigorating negative ions. You obviously can't get rid of the equipment (although photocopiers and printers, for example, should be kept in a separate room) but ask your manager to invest in an ionizer to compensate.

- If you find you suffer from itchy eyes or sore throats, the culprit may be low humidity. Humidity should be kept at 40 to 50 per cent.
- Natural ventilation is favourite but if the windows in your building are sealed, the air-conditioning filters should be regularly changed and cleaned.
- Ensure that the air is moving and that a supply of fresh air is available. Put fans on desks if there is no other alternative. Keep air grilles unblocked.
- Keep the office clean to reduce dust.
- Reduce static electricity by treating carpets with anti-static fluid.

Noise

- Noisy equipment such as printers and fax machines should be kept away from people's desks.
- Encourage colleagues to walk up to each other if they have something to say rather than shouting from one end of the room to the other.
- Try to find a quiet place to which you can retreat when you need to concentrate.
- Damp down noise as much as possible with covers, mats and screens.

Lighting

- Offices should be decorated in pale, matt colours to add light but cut glare.
- Place VDUs where glare from windows won't affect them. Put blinds or curtains on all windows so light levels can be adjusted. It also helps if workers have dimmer switches to give them control over lighting.
- Ensure there is no flickering from fluorescent lights.
- Use a desk spot lamp for close reading or detailed work.

Temperatures

The temperature should be kept between 20 and 24 °C: the legal minimum temperature is 16 °C. There is no legal maximum, but during a hot summer temperatures at work can become unbearable and make it hard to do anything productive. If your building isn't air-conditioned – and most British workplaces aren't – ask your employer to hire some portable air-conditioners if it gets really bad.

Feeling Fit

- Take regular exercise breaks, especially if you're deskbound. Walk about now and then. Do some simple stretching exercises – moving your head slowly round in a circle, shrugging shoulders up and down. Learn a few basic massage techniques. Don't hold your phone between shoulder and ear or you'll tense up your neck muscles and put your body out of alignment; hold the phone in your hand.
- If you're on your feet all day, take breaks to sit down and give them a rest.

VDU Advice

It's important for VDU users to take regular breaks. If you work too intensively on screen, you run the risk of eye strain and RSI (repetitive strain injury).

VDU users have a legal right to request eye tests at appropriate intervals and have them paid for by their employer. The employer is also obliged to pay for basic glasses if any vision defect is caused by VDU work.

Ensure that your work station is correctly set up by following these tips.

- *Keyboard.* Your arms should be at your side, relaxed, and your elbows should be a few inches from your body. Adjust chair and keyboard to minimize the distance you have to reach for the mouse. Position the keyboard so your arms can be held at an angle approximately 90° from your spine when you're sitting up straight. If you have to arch your wrists upward, you need to raise the chair or lower the keyboard stand.
- *Screen.* Your screen should be between 15° and 30° below the line created when you look straight ahead. If it is more than 30° lower, it may cause slouching. The distance between your eyes and the screen should be between 18 and 28 inches.
- *Chair.* The contours of your chair should follow the contours of your back. If you feel pressure on the tailbone, it's too low; if you feel pressure on your thighs, it's too high. The angle between your thighs and your spine should be at least 90°. Your thighs should be fully supported by the chair. Adjust the chair so that your feet are flat on the floor and your thighs parallel to it. If you have arm rests, use them to support your forearms as much as possible.
- *Light.* If your terminal faces a window, the glare of sunlight on it can be hard on your eyes: move the screen so it is perpendicular to the window, and use curtains, blinds or awnings. The American Optometric Association recommends that lighting for the office of a computer user should be about half the brightness level of normal office lighting. If the lighting in your office can't be adjusted, try unscrewing some bulbs – not forgetting to turn off the power first.

Chapter 23 / **The Importance of Image**

However good you are at your job, if your image is wrong it can hold you back. Other people make judgements from the way you look, dress, act and speak. Whatever the skills and talents you have underneath, it's what's on top that has the most immediate impact.

The Way You Look

If you want to be taken seriously at work, you have to look the part. Wacky clothes, tousled hair and teetering heels simply don't work if you want to get ahead. Neither do cutesy, little-girl clothes with lots of frills and fancy bits. If you think you're not advancing as quickly in your career as you should, or getting the respect you deserve, take a long look at the image you're projecting and see if there's room for improvement.

- Try to master the tricky balancing act of looking current and up-to-date without being too fashionable, serious without being stuffy. Stylish, chic and professional is the effect to aim for.
- Far more attention is paid to what women wear at work than what men wear – they can get away with the same suit day after day, but you can't. It may be unfair, it may be infuriating, but it's a fact and it would be naïve to ignore it. Your appearance is taken as an indicator of how you will perform your job: if you look as though you take time and care over the way you look, employers will assume you take the same time and care over your work. Always look well groomed.
- A jacket gives the impression of someone who's in charge.
- Ask friends and/or colleagues what kind of impression you

create at the moment, both good and bad points – as long as you're prepared for some surprises, not necessarily all pleasant. Once you know where you're falling down you can decide what steps to take.
- Every workplace has its own fashion code and the image that's most appropriate will vary from company to company. A casual look may work for a media environment but banking will call for a more sober approach. Make sure you match the company code.
- Ridiculous as it seems, some companies still aren't ready for women in trousers, so either you respect that or, if it makes you unhappy to wear skirts all the time, move to another employer where you feel more at ease.
- Make-up should be light and natural-looking, and should not clash with your outfit. Keep to neutral shades for your eyes, and matt lipsticks rather than gloss.
- Have regular manicures to keep your hands in shape.
- Have your hair cut regularly to keep it in shape. If you have long hair, ask your hairdresser to suggest different ways of wearing it up, which looks more professional than wearing it down. Don't ruin a tailored look by topping it with shaggy, unkempt hair. Hair swept up and off the face makes you appear more confident than if you hide behind a fringe.
- Shoes: stick to medium or flat heels. High heels won't be taken seriously. Have shoes regularly reheeled.
- Fitted skirts look smarter than floaty numbers.
- You can get away with tanned legs in summer, but otherwise you should always wear tights or stockings.
- Make sure everything is well pressed and ironed.
- Colour is important too. It's easy to stick to black or navy clothes but if you wear them all the time you run the risk of being ignored in the crowd. A touch of brighter colour will make you more visible.
- Certain things are pretty much guaranteed not to go down well wherever you work and the following are definite no-nos: acres of cleavage; matching blood-red lips and nails; evening clothes in the daytime; over-the-top make-up and jewellery; dousing yourself in perfume.

- Seriously short skirts and plunging necklines are out of place in the office. If you wear them to work, don't be surprised if people fail to take you seriously.
- Does the image you present tally with the real you or are you putting on a false front? Your image should complement your personality, not create a false impression.
- Look at other people and note what it is you like or dislike about their image, then consider how that relates to yourself, what hints you can take from people who impress you, what you can learn from people who've got it all wrong.
- Adapt your look and approach to suit the occasion, depending on whether you're with peers, clients, bosses, staff, etc.

How You Sound

Your voice plays a key role in affecting how other people perceive and treat you: nearly 40 per cent of the initial impression they form of you is based on the way you sound. Regardless of what you're saying, how you say it can make more impact – it's not *what* you say, but the *way* that you say it. If you've got your appearance right, why blow it the minute you open your mouth? A good speaking voice makes you appear more authoritative, confident and powerful. Actors and politicians pay great attention to their voices, realizing how deeply they affect the message they're trying to put across.

- No one responds well to a shrill voice so try to pitch your voice low.
- Speak slowly and articulately. Don't slur or mumble; leave pauses between sentences, instead of rushing everything out.
- Speak up – a quiet, shy, little-girly voice won't do you any favours. It's hard to judge how loud your own voice is (it sounds louder to you than to others) so ask friends what they think.
- There's nothing wrong with a regional accent, but if yours is particularly broad, make an effort to speak slowly to help people understand you.

- Avoid raising your inflection at the end of sentences, making statements sound like questions and giving the impression you're unsure of what you're saying.
- Avoid tagging on 'isn't it?' 'don't you agree?' etc. at the end of your sentences. Again, it gives the impression you're not entirely sure about what you're saying. Too many umms and ers give the same impression of vagueness and lack of confidence.
- If you're doubtful about how your voice comes across, try recording yourself then listen and try to judge it objectively to find out where you're falling down.
- Good posture is crucial for good speech: rounded shoulders and high heels can all have an adverse effect on your voice. If you stand up when making important telephone calls, it will make you sound more authoritative.
- Avoid too many qualifying words – really interesting, very, very exciting, etc. sounds little-girly and unbusinesslike.
- It's all too easy for your voice to give away underlying emotions of lack of confidence, fear or anger: too many short breaths when you're nervous, high-pitched squeaks when you argue.
- Poor posture – slumping or hunching your shoulders – weakens your voice, as do tight clothes which restrict your breathing.
- Looking down as you speak will prevent you projecting your voice properly.
- Open your mouth when you speak – you can't speak clearly if you're barely parting your lips. Imagining that someone is trying to lip-read what you're saying will help you to articulate.

Chapter 24 / **Business Travel and Entertaining**

Travelling on Business

More and more women are being called upon to travel for their work, both at home and, as the business world becomes increasingly international, abroad. At first it sounds great fun but once the novelty of satellite TV and a mini bar in your hotel room wears off, you may feel lonely and isolated. Add to that pitying waiters, over-interested fellow diners and some airline or hotel staff giving priority to male travellers, and the travelling businesswoman can start to feel really got at.

Learning to behave more assertively (see chapter 16) can take care of some of the problems, and careful planning will make the whole experience of going on a business trip less stressful.
- Look for hotels with single-woman-friendly policies – locks and peepholes on bedroom doors, receptionists who don't shout out room numbers for strange men to overhear, rooms close to lifts, etc.
- If you go to the same cities regularly, try to stay in the same place so that you get to know the people and feel more at home.
- The more you can plan in advance the better. Keep a checklist of things to be done, such as booking transport, accommodation, car hire, insurance, itinerary, foreign currency and travellers' cheques, and start ticking them off as soon as you can, rather than resorting to last-minute panic.
- If you have to travel frequently to far-flung places, keep your vaccinations up to date as a matter of course, rather than waiting until you get the call.
- Check what's covered under your company travel insurance

and consider taking out your own annual frequent-traveller policy on top of that.
- Always leave a copy of your itinerary with someone in the office, together with a contact number at work where you can be reached in an emergency.
- Don't forget to pack the essentials: passport; tickets; insurance certificate; hotel-booking confirmation; money; itinerary; maps and guides; first-aid kit; names and addresses of contacts; papers and documents; pens.
- Check that you know where you're going. Will you be met on arrival? If you're driving, do you need a map?
- When you're drawing up an itinerary, don't try to fit in too much and allow yourself plenty of time to travel between appointments.
- Find out what social events will be built into your itinerary, and how formal they will be, so that you don't get caught out without the right clothes.
- When flying, try, if possible, to take only carry-on luggage on the plane, so that all your planning doesn't turn to disaster when your case goes astray. At the very least, keep all the most important things in your hand luggage – toiletries, documents and a few clean clothes.
- When deciding what form of transport to use, bear in mind that travelling by train or plane gives you the chance to read or prepare for your meeting; driving doesn't – but you're more in control of where you go and when.
- Make sure people know who is handling your work in your absence.
- When you're going abroad, bone up on the culture of the country you're visiting so you don't make any terrible *faux pas*. You may not agree with its citizens' attitude towards women but a business trip isn't the time to try to change the cultural perceptions and traditions of a nation.
- Be just as safety-conscious as you would at home. Some people seem to abandon all sensible precautions the minute they're abroad.

- If you're nervous about dining alone, read a book or newspaper.
- Avoid making unnecessary eye contact with strange men who might interpret it as a come-on.
- In countries where single women are the subject of suspicion and disapproval wear a wedding ring even if you're not married.
- Carry a rubber doorstop to wedge under your hotel room door to keep it shut.
- If you don't like your room, or aren't convinced that it's secure enough, ask to be moved to another.

Work-related Socializing

- At business receptions and parties, don't stick to one person all night – you have to circulate. It's hard at first, but the more you do it, the more people you'll know at the next function.
- Don't feel you have to go to every single event to which you're invited but make an effort to attend some, if you don't want to be seen as stand-offish or uninterested and not a team player.
- If you've said you'll go to an event, always turn up. If you're not going to be able to make it, let the host know.
- If you're taking a business contact to lunch, find out in advance if your guest has any preferences about food (vegetarian?), non-smoking tables, etc. Always remember your credit card and arrive early so you'll be there to welcome them: it's extremely rude to leave them sitting on their own.
- If you can, choose a restaurant where the staff know you and explain before the meal that the bill should come to you. Too many places still automatically hand it to a man.
- After work, drinks with colleagues can be a great way to wind down, relieve the stress of work and form bonds. But be sensible: don't drink too much and don't try to keep up with the lads. Avoid gossiping – in a more relaxed setting, and after a few drinks, it can be easy to give more away than you normally would or should.
- If you find people try to press more alcohol on you than you want, tell them that you're on antibiotics or you're driving.

Chapter 25 / Setting Up Your Own Business

Who hasn't dreamt at times of setting up their own business? When you're fed up with the nine-to-five routine, sick of office politics and feeling overworked and under-appreciated by your boss, there's obvious appeal in the idea of going it alone.

Working for yourself has all sorts of attractions – such as being able to decide what you do and when, having no one but yourself to answer to and the satisfaction of working towards something in which you're really interested. However, it also means saying goodbye to regular routine and the security of a regular pay packet, and you'll probably find yourself working harder than ever before.

If you thrive on challenge and you're not afraid to take risks, though, becoming your own boss could be the best move you ever make. Start by researching your idea through and through: setting up alone is a risk, but make sure it's a calculated one.

Have You Got What It Takes?

To be a successful entrepreneur, you need certain personal skills and aptitudes so, before you go any further, take a long, hard look at yourself to see if you possess these essential qualities.
• Adaptability: to start with, you'll probably be your own sales-force and secretary as well as your own boss.
• Drive and determination: success rarely happens overnight.
• Financial acumen: you don't have to be a wizard accountant, but you need some financial nous to survive.

- Confidence and enthusiasm: the more you have, the more you'll inspire it in others.
- Positive attitude: can you bounce back from setbacks?
- Selling ability: it's no good having a wonderful product or service if you can't get other people to buy it.
- Good health: there's no paid sick leave when you're self-employed.
- Self-motivation: will you be able to get the job done without someone else to drive you along?

There are other factors to consider, too. Are you prepared to accept a lower standard of living to start with? Think, too, about whether you'd be happy working alone. You might moan about the people you work with but once you no longer have an office full of colleagues you may find you miss them. One way to fill the gap is to join a local small business support network so that you can get to know other people in the same situation. Your local Chamber of Commerce or some of the organizations listed under 'Where to Go for Help' (p. 136) should be able to give you contact numbers for support groups in your area. Supportive family, friends and partners are very important, too.

What Sort of Business?

Reckon you do have what it takes to succeed? Then the next step is to decide what sort of business to go for.

If you find a gap in the market, starting a business from scratch may lead to the greatest financial rewards – but it is also the riskiest option. You might feel happier buying into an established business instead, or improving on an existing service.

Franchising – where you pay for the right to use the name of a company (for example Body Shop or Pizza Express) and sell its products or services – is an increasingly popular option. It means less independence and more limited scope but the advantages are that you have a tried and tested formula and support from the franchisor. And statistics show a greater success rate for franchises than for other small business start-ups. Find out exactly what you will get for your initial investment (which can be anything from £3,000 upwards) and what percentage of turnover you'll have to pay the franchisor. Most banks have franchise departments that will advise you on whether the one you're considering is a sound option or not, and the British Franchise Association (01491 578049) will supply an information sheet.

Don't worry if you can't come up with a wonderful new idea for a business: most new businesses are a variation on an old theme or a continuation of a successful formula. Flick through *Yellow Pages* or business directories to get ideas of the sorts of businesses around. Think about what the current growth areas are and whether they're likely to continue to grow or to decline. Would you like to do something based on skills you use in your current job, such as foreign languages, organizing events or teaching music? Or do you have any hobbies that could be developed into a business? Make a list of your interests and think about their business potential. Ask your friends for their ideas of what you can do: they may pick up on something you hadn't thought of.

Research the Market

Once you've decided going it alone is right for you and you have some ideas about the type of business you want to go for, it's time for some market research. Identify your competitors and their strengths and weaknesses. If there isn't any competition, ask yourself why not: there may be a genuine gap in the market or simply no demand. Think about what will make your product better than that of your rivals; for example, better prices, a faster service, longer opening hours.

Pricing is important: people make certain assumptions according to what something costs so how much will you charge? Look at your competitors' prices to get a starting point and remember to take into account all your overheads.

Be clear about who your target customers are: their age, sex, occupation, interests, income, etc. Where do they live? Are they corporate or domestic clients? Will demand be steady or seasonal?

Promotion

No matter how wonderful your product, people can't buy it if they don't know about it, so how will you attract their attention? Advertising isn't cheap so if you decide to follow this route, make sure you target properly: a small trade paper might be more appropriate and attract more custom than an ad in a large-circulation general-interest paper. There are other avenues to explore too, such as attracting passing custom with inventive window displays or boards outside premises, distributing leaflets round local houses, businesses or cars. You could try for free publicity by sending an attention-grabbing press release to your local paper, radio station or a relevant trade journal. Volunteer to talk at conferences or write articles for the trade press. Consider taking a stand at trade exhibitions or fairs.

Word-of-mouth is an important way of finding new clients, too: do each job well, don't let people down – and they will recommend you to others.

Finding Premises

Where will you carry out your business? Working from home means fewer overheads and no commuting but check that your lease or mortgage conditions allow it. You may need planning permission (for example, if the business is noisy or will cause traffic congestion); ask your local authority's planning department. And tell your insurance company what you're doing or you may find your household insurance is invalidated. If you're using your car for business purposes you may need extra insurance on that too.

If you want to buy or rent premises, check them out thoroughly. Location is especially important for a retail outlet or restaurant, so visit at different times of day to check out passing trade. Is the site close to transport routes? What are the parking facilities like? Are there other popular retailers nearby who will attract shoppers? Ask the local authority if there are any plans for the area that will affect the business: for example, are they building a bypass that will divert custom away from a busy restaurant?

Legal and Financial Aspects

And so to the practicalities of how your business will run. There are a host of nitty-gritty details to be considered, but these are some of the most important.
- Are there any legal requirements with which you must comply? Many businesses (restaurants, employment agencies, pet shops, etc.) need a licence to trade. And it's no good setting up a home catering business if your kitchen doesn't meet health and safety standards.
- What legal status will your business take? Will you operate as a sole trader (the simplest form), a limited company, a partnership or a co-operative? Your answer to this question will have legal and financial implications so take professional advice before you decide.
- What will you call your business? If you're a company, there are certain restrictions: for example, no two companies can have the same name and there are some words (such as international and council) that you're not allowed to use without proper authority. Companies House in Cardiff (01222 380801) has a free leaflet, *Choosing a Company Name*, plus other advice notes for start-ups.
- If you plan to take on other staff, find out about your responsibilities as an employer. Jobcentres (listed under Employment Service in the phone book) can give advice; and ACAS, too, provides leaflets on employment issues (call 01455 852225 for details).
- Being self-employed will affect your tax and National Insurance, so you must tell the Inland Revenue and DSS what you're doing. Your local Tax Enquiry Centre (in the phone book under Inland

Revenue) can give advice; they also have a free video and booklet called *Getting Tax Right from the Start.*
- If you think your gross turnover will go above a certain amount (£47,000 in the 1996/7 tax year), you must register for VAT. Under that amount, you can register voluntarily, which allows you to reclaim VAT on anything you buy for business use but it also makes your book-keeping more complicated!
- Find an accountant and solicitor. Under the Law Society's Lawyers for Business scheme you get free initial consultation with a solicitor; call the answerphone service on 0171-405 9075 for details. When you're looking for an accountant, try to choose one with experience of working with clients in a similar field and make sure he or she is a member of the Institute of Chartered Accountants or the Chartered Association of Certified Accountants. Ask around for recommendations or call the ICA (0171-920 8100) for a list of chartered accountants in your area.

Putting Together a Business Plan

Once you've done all the research, it's down to the all-important task of drawing up a business plan. This is basically a question of pulling together all the information you've gathered so far and making certain projections based on that information. Your plan will include details of your business: its personnel, its objectives, your product and its market, information on how it will operate and, most importantly, a financial forecast. The purpose is to show potential investors – your bank manager, for example – what your business is and how it will work so that they can assess whether or not it's worth investing in. Putting things down on paper also forces you to think them through in an organized manner.

Keep your plan simple and as concise as possible; illustrate it with charts and other graphics, if it helps. Be realistic rather than optimistic about your projections, and if you know there will be obstacles, acknowledge them and explain how you intend to overcome them. Be prepared to explain and justify all your projections.

Your business plan is vital to your chances of getting financial backing, so devote some time and effort to getting it right. Most of the agencies mentioned under 'Where to Go for Help' (see p. 136) will give guidance on putting a plan together – some even supply pre-printed forms which make it easier for you – so ask them for help.

Finding the Funding

Armed with your completed business plan, you're ready to approach possible sources of finance. This is a major hurdle but if you've put in enough time and thought you should be ready for it. Schemes such as the Prince's Youth Business Trust are aimed specifically at people who don't have other sources of funds. Other investors may expect you to put up some of your own money.

You might find friends and family willing to invest in your business, too, but if you do borrow money from people you know, make sure that they can afford to lend it and draw up a clear agreement about how and when you will pay it back: it's all too easy to lose friends through disagreements over money.

How to Survive

Many small businesses fail within the first two years, and only half of new businesses survive more than five, so it's obvious that your problems aren't all over once you're up and running.

On the financial front, you need to keep complete records to satisfy the tax office but it's also in your own interests to stay on top of your business and see where it's going by keeping a careful track of your finances at all times. As you go along, refer back to your original goals and cashflow projections to see how you're performing against them. That way, if things go wrong, you can spot it at an early stage and take appropriate action.

Where to Go for Help

- All the major banks provide advice and information on starting up and possible grant sources. NatWest, for example, has an excellent free booklet, *The Business Start-Up Guide*, and a small business adviser in every high-street branch.
- Training and Enterprise Councils (known as Local Enterprise Companies in Scotland) provide information, advice and counselling, though at the time of going to press they were unable to offer any financial support. Find your local TEC under Training and Enterprise Council in the phone book, or call the TEC National Council on 0171-735 0010.
- Local Enterprise Agencies (Enterprise Trusts in Scotland) supply information and advice, especially on developing your business plan, and can put you in touch with sources of financial support. Call Business in the Community on 0171-224 1600 to find your LEA.
- The Department of Trade and Industry's Business Link scheme is a government service offering help and advice to small businesses. It is aimed at businesses that are already up and running rather than at start-ups. Call Freefone 0800 500 200 for details of the business information and support services they offer and for a contact number for your local Business Link.
- Livewire helps 16–25-year-olds start their own business. They can supply a free copy of their *Could This Be You?* booklet and put you in touch with a business adviser to help you research your idea, produce a business plan and look for funding. They also run the annual Business Start Up Awards, which reward well-researched business plans with cash prizes and help in kind. Write to Livewire, Freepost, Newcastle upon Tyne NE1 1BR or call their hotline number 0345 573252.
- The Prince's Youth Business Trust offers advice and finance (in the form of grants or low-interest loans) to 18–29-year-old would-be entrepreneurs who are unable to find funding elsewhere. Find your regional office by calling Freefone 0800 842 842 or, in Scot-

land, contact the Prince's Scottish Youth Business Trust on 0141-248 4999.
- Instant Muscle (in England and Wales) runs free business planning courses and specializes in one-to-one counselling to provide business advice over an extended period. They don't provide loans or grants and exist to help unemployed people only. Call 0171-603 2604 to find your local branch.

Chapter 26 / **Changing Career**

Gone are the days when you left school, went straight into a job and stayed at the same company until you got the gold watch fifty years later. Nowadays you're almost looked on as slightly odd if you stay in one place for very long. The idea of changing not just job but your whole career direction has become much more accepted.

This is partly down to the effect of rapid technological advances and economic recessions, which have forced consequent changes in employment patterns. We're effectively undergoing another industrial revolution, with a growth in the numbers of people working freelance, on short-term contracts or part time. It's increasingly common for people to reassess their career and whole way of life once they get into their thirties. Maybe they find the high-flying career they were pursuing has become less important to them than more free time or better quality of life.

Time for a Change?

Working out whether or not you really need to change is a complicated decision and needs lots of thought. Consider the following statements. If too many strike a chord, then yes, you probably are ready for a change.
- You feel ashamed or embarrassed when people ask you what you do for a living.
- You haven't learned anything new in the past year or two.
- You feel tired all the time.
- You've grown and changed since you joined the company but everyone still has you pigeon-holed as the person you were when you first started there.

- You never meet any new and interesting people in the course of your day-to-day life.
- You've had your eye on a particular job for a while but others have been promoted ahead of you.
- You haven't fulfilled your ambitions and goals and now you've lost sight of what they were.
- Office politics often get in the way of you doing your job.
- You sometimes ring in sick even when you know you're not really ill.
- You've lost interest in your job and do only the bare minimum to get by.
- You feel that you're not using your skills to the full.
- You are constantly moaning about work to your friends and partner.
- You feel as if you just don't fit in and you frequently argue with your colleagues.
- You experience feelings of panic or depression on the way to work, especially on Monday mornings.
- You never mix socially with any of your colleagues.
- You hate the amount of commuting you have to do.
- It's a real struggle trying to make ends meet on your current income.
- The company doesn't have a track record of promoting people and you can see no obvious next step up the career ladder.
- The skills you use or have acquired in your job wouldn't be of any use anywhere else.
- You can't remember the last time you felt stretched or challenged at work.
- You know that other people doing a similar job in other organizations have greater job satisfaction and bigger salaries.

What to Change to

It may be that a small change is all you need: perhaps you don't need a whole new career, but just increased responsibility, shorter hours, more flexibility, more money. Would you like a sabbatical, a job share, a career break? Would a promotion in your current company keep you happy or is it time to move to another organization?

Write down on paper the pros and cons of staying with your current employer, for example:

Pros
The company is expanding into new directions and will be looking for staff for its new divisions.
Other people who have left seem to regret it.
The company offers excellent staff training opportunities.
You're still learning things in your job.

Cons
The company is selling to a competitor with a worse reputation for staff welfare.
Women don't seem to make it to the higher levels of the company.
Commuting to work takes too much time out of your day.
Your way up is blocked by a superior who's been in the job for years and shows no signs of leaving.

If you're nervous of change, it's better to opt for a new job within the same field rather than a complete change of direction; that way you can capitalize on your existing contacts, knowledge and experience. Starting totally afresh is altogether more alarming and much harder work. Explore related careers first. Write down your current job on a piece of paper and around that write all the other people you deal with in the course of your work. A journalist, for example, might deal with public-relations consultants, advertising sales people, marketing advisers, designers, printers, etc. Could you move into one of these areas?

If no related jobs appeal and you realize that what you really need is a total career change, then deciding what to change *to* can be the hardest part of career planning. Don't panic or make the mistake of rushing into something, anything, just to get away from where you are now. Change *to* something you want, not just *from* something you hate. Enjoying your work shouldn't be a luxury but a basic: there has to be something about it you like or appreciate to give you the energy and enthusiasm to keep going.

Let yourself dream to start with: if you could be or do anything, what would it be? To help clarify things in your mind, think back over your life and make a note of all the times when you felt most truly happy and the things you've done that have given you most satisfaction. A theme may begin to emerge which is different from what you imagined. You may discover, for instance, that there are areas within your leisure activities that appeal to you and suggest other job possibilities: you might have helped someone to read and write as part of a literacy programme and found that you enjoy instructing people. What you are is determined by your entire life, not just the work portion.

If it is a complete change you're after you may be frightened, but doing as much research as possible into your new direction before you go for it is the key to minimizing fear of failure. Go back to the starting-out section of this book for ideas of how to choose which way to go and how to go about getting there, and chapter 20 for tips on drawing up a career plan.

Remember that some changes may be forced upon you rather than chosen – as a result of redundancy, relocation, divorce, etc. So, given that it's safe to assume most of us will undergo a change of direction at some point, it makes sense to try to anticipate the future and make sure that it won't come as a shock. Keep an eye on future trends and how they might affect you. You have to be adaptable and ride *with* changes rather than fighting against them. Keeping pace means keeping your skills as up-to-date as possible and acquiring as many transferable skills as you can. It's an ongoing process: the more you continue to adjust and improve your skills, the better your chances of staying ahead.

Visit Penguin on the Internet
and browse at your leisure

- preview sample extracts of our forthcoming books
- read about your favourite authors
- investigate over 10,000 titles
- enter one of our literary quizzes
- win some fantastic prizes in our competitions
- e-mail us with your comments and book reviews
- instantly order any Penguin book

and masses more!

'To be recommended without reservation ... a rich and rewarding on-line experience' – Internet Magazine

www.penguin.co.uk

READ MORE IN PENGUIN

In every corner of the world, on every subject under the sun, Penguin represents quality and variety – the very best in publishing today.

For complete information about books available from Penguin – including Puffins, Penguin Classics and Arkana – and how to order them, write to us at the appropriate address below. Please note that for copyright reasons the selection of books varies from country to country.

In the United Kingdom: Please write to *Dept. EP, Penguin Books Ltd, Bath Road, Harmondsworth, West Drayton, Middlesex UB7 ODA*

In the United States: Please write to *Consumer Sales, Penguin USA, P.O. Box 999, Dept. 17109, Bergenfield, New Jersey 07621-0120*. VISA and MasterCard holders call 1-800-253-6476 to order Penguin titles

In Canada: Please write to *Penguin Books Canada Ltd, 10 Alcorn Avenue, Suite 300, Toronto, Ontario M4V 3B2*

In Australia: Please write to *Penguin Books Australia Ltd, P.O. Box 257, Ringwood, Victoria 3134*

In New Zealand: Please write to *Penguin Books (NZ) Ltd, Private Bag 102902, North Shore Mail Centre, Auckland 10*

In India: Please write to *Penguin Books India Pvt Ltd, 706 Eros Apartments, 56 Nehru Place, New Delhi 110 019*

In the Netherlands: Please write to *Penguin Books Netherlands bv, Postbus 3507, NL-1001 AH Amsterdam*

In Germany: Please write to *Penguin Books Deutschland GmbH, Metzlerstrasse 26, 60594 Frankfurt am Main*

In Spain: Please write to *Penguin Books S. A., Bravo Murillo 19, 1° B, 28015 Madrid*

In Italy: Please write to *Penguin Italia s.r.l., Via Felice Casati 20, I-20124 Milano*

In France: Please write to *Penguin France S. A., 17 rue Lejeune, F-31000 Toulouse*

In Japan: Please write to *Penguin Books Japan, Ishikiribashi Building, 2-5-4, Suido, Bunkyo-ku, Tokyo 112*

In South Africa: Please write to *Longman Penguin Southern Africa (Pty) Ltd, Private Bag X08, Bertsham 2013*

READ MORE IN PENGUIN

REFERENCE

The Penguin Dictionary of Literary Terms and Literary Theory
J. A. Cuddon

'Scholarly, succinct, comprehensive and entertaining, this is an important book, an indispensable work of reference. It draws on the literature of many languages and quotes aptly and freshly from our own' – *The Times Educational Supplement*

The Penguin Dictionary of Symbols
Jean Chevalier and Alain Gheerbrant, translated by John Buchanan-Brown

This book draws together folklore, literary and artistic sources and focuses on the symbolic dimension of every colour, number, sound, gesture, expression or character trait that has benefited from symbolic interpretation.

Roget's Thesaurus of English Words and Phrases
Edited by Betty Kirkpatrick

This new edition of Roget's classic work, now brought up to date for the nineties, will increase anyone's command of the English language. Fully cross-referenced, it includes synonyms of every kind (formal or colloquial, idiomatic and figurative) for almost 900 headings. It is a must for writers and utterly fascinating for any English speaker.

The Penguin Guide to Synonyms and Related Words
S. I. Hayakawa

'More helpful than a thesaurus, more humane than a dictionary, the *Guide to Synonyms and Related Words* maps linguistic boundaries with precision, sensitivity to nuance and, on occasion, dry wit' – *The Times Literary Supplement*

The Penguin Book of Exotic Words Janet Whitcut

English is the most widely used language today, its unusually rich vocabulary the result of new words from all over the world being freely assimilated into the language. With entries arranged thematically, words of Saxon, Viking, French, Latin, Greek, Hebrew, Arabic and Indian origin are explored in this fascinating book.

READ MORE IN PENGUIN

REFERENCE

Medicines: A Guide for Everybody Peter Parish

Now in its seventh edition and completely revised and updated, this bestselling guide is written in ordinary language for the ordinary reader yet will prove indispensable to anyone involved in health care – nurses, pharmacists, opticians, social workers and doctors.

Media Law Geoffrey Robertson QC and Andrew Nichol

Crisp and authoritative surveys explain the up-to-date position on defamation, obscenity, official secrecy, copyright and confidentiality, contempt of court, the protection of privacy and much more.

The Penguin Careers Guide
Anna Alston and Anne Daniel; Consultant Editor: Ruth Miller

As the concept of a 'job for life' wanes, this guide encourages you to think broadly about occupational areas as well as describing day-to-day work and detailing the latest developments and qualifications such as NVQs. Special features include possibilities for working part-time and job-sharing, returning to work after a break and an assessment of the current position of women.

The Penguin Dictionary of Troublesome Words Bill Bryson

Why should you avoid discussing the *weather conditions*? Can a married woman be celibate? Why is it eccentric to talk about the aroma of a cowshed? A straightforward guide to the pitfalls and hotly disputed issues in standard written English.

The Penguin Dictionary of Musical Performers Arthur Jacobs

In this invaluable companion volume to *The Penguin Dictionary of Music* Arthur Jacobs has brought together the names of over 2,500 performers. Music is written by composers, yet it is the interpreters who bring it to life; in this comprehensive book they are at last given their due.

READ MORE IN PENGUIN

BUSINESS AND ECONOMICS

Trust Francis Fukuyama

'The man who made his name proclaiming the end of history when communism collapsed has now re-entered the lists, arguing that free markets, competition and hard work are *not* the sole precursors for prosperity. There is another key ingredient – trust ... This is the heart of Fukuyama's theory ... it is both important and full of insight' – *Guardian*

I am Right – You are Wrong Edward de Bono

Edward de Bono expects his ideas to outrage conventional thinkers, yet time has been on his side, and the ideas that he first put forward twenty years ago are now accepted mainstream thinking. Here, in this brilliantly argued assault on outmoded thought patterns, he calls for nothing less than a New Renaissance.

Lloyds Bank Small Business Guide Sara Williams

This long-running guide to making a success of your small business deals with real issues in a practical way. 'As comprehensive an introduction to setting up a business as anyone could need' – *Daily Telegraph*

The Road Ahead Bill Gates

Bill Gates – the man who built Microsoft – takes us back to when he dropped out of Harvard to start his own software company and discusses how we stand on the brink of a new technology revolution that will for ever change and enhance the way we buy, work, learn and communicate with each other.

Exploring Management Across the World David J. Hickson

This companion volume to *Management Worldwide* contains selections from seminal writings on centralization, individualism, work relationships, power and risk among managers and countries and cultures all over the globe.

Understanding Organizations Charles B. Handy

Of practical as well as theoretical interest, this book shows how general concepts can help solve specific organizational problems.

READ MORE IN PENGUIN

BUSINESS AND ECONOMICS

In with the Euro, Out with the Pound Christopher Johnson

The European Union is committed to setting up the Euro as a single currency, yet Britain has held back, with both politicians and public unable to make up their minds. In this timely, convincing analysis, Christopher Johnson asserts that this 'wait and see' policy is damaging and will result in far less favourable entry terms.

Lloyds Bank Tax Guide Sara Williams and John Willman

An average employee tax bill is over £4,000 a year. But how much time do you spend checking it? Four out of ten never check the bill – and most spend less than an hour. Mistakes happen. This guide can save YOU money. 'An unstuffy read, packed with sound information' – *Observer*

The Penguin Companion to European Union
Timothy Bainbridge with Anthony Teasdale

A balanced, comprehensive picture of the institutions, personalities, arguments and political pressures that have shaped Europe since the end of the Second World War.

Understanding Offices Joanna Eley and Alexi F. Marmot

Few companies systematically treat space as a scarce resource or make conscious efforts to get the best from their buildings. This book offers guidance on image, safety, comfort, amenities, energy-efficiency, value for money and much more.

Faith and Credit Susan George and Fabrizio Sabelli

In its fifty years of existence, the World Bank has influenced more lives in the Third World than any other institution, yet remains largely unknown, even enigmatic. This richly illuminating and lively overview examines the policies of the Bank, its internal culture and the interests it serves.

READ MORE IN PENGUIN

Cosmopolitan Career Guides: a series of lively and practical handbooks produced by *Cosmopolitan* writers on a wide range of subjects.

***Cosmopolitan* Guide to Working in Journalism and Publishing**
Suzanne King

Careers in journalism and publishing are seen as highly desirable, but what exactly do they involve? Suzanne King describes the work undertaken by those in all sections of the industries, from newspaper reporter to magazine editor, TV researcher to radio PA, book commissioning editor to freelance writer. This expert guide also lists relevant training schemes and courses, salary ranges and numerous case histories, providing inspiration, insider information and invaluable advice.

***Cosmopolitan* Guide to Working in Retail**
Elaine Robertson

The retailing business is the country's biggest employer, providing jobs for one in ten of the UK workforce. What kind of career opportunities can retail offer you? From window dresser to buyer, personal shopper to department manager, this informative book will help you choose the right career.

READ MORE IN PENGUIN

Cosmopolitan Career Guides: a series of lively and practical handbooks produced by *Cosmopolitan* writers on a wide range of subjects.

Cosmopolitan Guide to Working in PR and Advertising
Robert Gray and Julia Hobsbawm

What does a career in PR or advertising involve? Which job is best for you? Robert Gray looks at the various jobs in advertising agencies, from account handling and planning to copywriting and creative services. He also examines the options for a career in advertising on the client side and highlights the opportunities for breaking into media buying or media sales and the sort of vacancies that exist in this fast-moving field. Julia Hobsbawm looks at the different kinds of public relations and explains how the industry works. She describes what's involved in working for a consultancy or in-house department on projects ranging from media networking and issuing press releases to crisis management and celebrity publicity.

Cosmopolitan Guide to Working in Finance
Robert Gray

What opportunities can a career in finance offer you? In clear and straightforward terms, this guide describes the different jobs in finance and outlines the qualities and qualifications you'll need to make it in each one. From accountancy to insurance broking, fund management to investment analysis, High Street banking to international currency trading, this informative book will help you choose the right career. It also lists relevant courses and training opportunities and is illustrated throughout with helpful case histories of women working in finance, who talk about the pleasures and drawbacks of their jobs.

published or forthcoming:

Cosmopolitan Guide to Student Life
Louise Clark
Cosmopolitan Guide to to the Big Trip
Elaine Robertson and Suzanne King